Praise for *The 7 Secrets of Money*

'The 7 Secrets of Money is an essential read for anyone currently investing for their future or considering doing so. It provides a simple, yet powerful, framework for making better investment decisions, avoiding the common mistakes that investors make, and simplifying what needs to be done in practice. Not reading this book will be a costly mistake.'

Tim Hale, author of *Smarter Investing*,
MD, Albion Strategic Consulting

'If you've ever wondered why your portfolio only rises 5% when the markets rise 10%, then this book is for you. You can make your money work harder for you (rather than for others), and you can do it without having to take any greater risks. This book is a must-read for all of us who want to retire with a sense of financial security. Get the strategy right, avoid giving your money away inadvertently, don't take unnecessary risks, and learn how to enjoy your hard-earned income. The authors of this book help you achieve all these objectives in a clear and readily understood manner. I cannot recommend it enough.'

Mark Baldry, private investor and
Senior Consultant, Priorities for Profit

'*The 7 Secrets of Money* is an easy-to-read guide to how investment works, where the costs arise, what to avoid, and how to choose a financial adviser. Having read this book, the reader will understand the implications of the advice given, and be in a position to make an informed contribution to the decision making process.'

Janice Trebble,
Partner at Saunders and Dolleymore LLP

'For many years an ever-widening chasm has been growing between individuals and the vast, confusing machine that is the global financial system. This book and the individuals behind it provide a bridge in a readable and comprehensible manner, at once debunking many of the myths and pseudo-science which bedevil finance and at the same time recognising that financial planning is as variable as people themselves. To read this book will take only an hour or so, but it may well be rewarded by a lifetime of contentment and will certainly convince the reader that the fools' gold still peddled far too often by the financial establishment only leads to inevitable disappointment.'

Paul Bradshaw,
chairman of Nucleus Financial Group

The 7 Secrets of Money

2nd edition

The insider's guide to personal investment success

Simon Brown | Ben Sherwood | Richard Stott | Bruce Wilson

The 7 Secrets of Money: The insider's guide to personal investment success, 2nd edition

First published in Great Britain in 2011 by HotHive Books, Evesham, UK

This second edition published by SRA Books in 2013

A CIP catalogue record for this book is available from the British Library.

ISBN 978-1-909116-02-3

eISBN 978-1-908342-05-8

Project managed and edited by Sonja Jefferson
www.valuablecontent.co.uk
Editorial consultant: Paul Forty at Brookes Forty, www.brookesforty.com
Website development by Inspire, www.inspiredc.co.uk
Text design by Daniel Penfold
Typeset in Garamond & Scala Sans by Daniel Penfold
Printed and bound in the UK by TJ International, Padstow

Disclaimer

www.7secretsofmoney.co.uk

'It is always from a minority acting in ways
different from what the majority would prescribe
that the majority in the end learns to do better.'

Friedrich August von Hayek,
Nobel Prize winning economist[1]

Contents

Figures

Foreword

When historians of the future look back at the 21st century, they will see it as the beginning of a golden age of finance, where the central purpose and function of financial products, financial institutions, financial information and foremost of all financial advisers comes to be understood as the delivery of freedom into the lives of people. *The 7 Secrets of Money* deserves a place at the heart of that movement.

In the 20th century finance was all about product, and therefore sales. The 21st century, starting as it did with a collapse in equity markets, a banking crisis and unprecedented regulatory change, looks to be all about the consumer. But that is a misnomer. The very term 'consumer' is still in the old model. It implies consumption of product and therefore still sales. In contrast, the authors' passion for truth in investing, and for client-centred advice, practically leaps off every page of *The 7 Secrets*.

Lost still in the shadow of the century of 'sales', we still fail to comprehend that money is the facilitator of each of our individual lives of choice; it is about us and our freedom, not about gambling, nor untoward profits of greedy advisers or powerful corporations. We are still in disbelief that there are advisers dedicated primarily to bring us that freedom. Brown, Sherwood, Stott and Wilson give the lie to our disbelief.

As each of us addresses our dreams of freedom, three domains of investigation are crucial. Life planning explores and identifies the heart of our concerns, passions and aspirations. Financial planning delivers it, addressing all of the practical financial needs of a person, from budget to investment to insurance and estate planning, retirement and taxes. Investments are the third domain, critical to the delivery of our aspirations, but investments are also the area of our greatest distrust. *The 7 Secrets* goes a long way to explain why and gives us a new template to work from.

There is wisdom here at the core. Keep your costs low (including taxes and fees of all kinds), keep your aspirations clear, diversify your risks and aim for the best rate of return within your risk level. Reading *The 7 Secrets of Money*, one realises there is a science and a logic to investing. Relief, trust and exhilaration replace confusion, lethargy and distrust.

This book describes an investment methodology that has been adopted by many of the elite, the most educated and highly qualified financial planners in the US, the UK and Australia. Read it and see why!

George Kinder,
author of *The Seven Stages of Money Maturity* and
Lighting the Torch and founder of the
Kinder Institute of Life Planning

www.kinderinstitute.com

Introduction

Become a better investor

The 7 Secrets of Money has something new and controversial to say about managing your money. For too long the financial establishment has put its own interests above the needs of individual investors. The result is a consistent failure to deliver the returns that you need to meet your life goals.

We want this situation to change. In this book we show you how to take control of your finances and put your interests first. We will demystify the investment process and reveal the truth about money. We will give you the knowledge and tools you need to become a better investor. The route to success is simpler than you would expect.

In *The 7 Secrets of Money* we break down the barriers, exploding the myths around finance and investment, exposing the secrets to success that the financial establishment has for too long kept to itself, and provide you with the investing success you deserve.

Conventional advice has served us badly

The financial establishment has deliberately encouraged ideas such as investing in 'superstar' managers, stock picking, market timing and jumping for the latest 'innovative' product in an attempt to beat the market.

Conventional approaches such as these better serve the interests of those people manufacturing and selling the products, rather than furnishing investors with the returns you need to reach your goals.

This type of advice has resulted in huge disappointment for the vast majority of investors:

- Many investors are devastated when they realise that their savings have not grown enough to meet their financial goals or, even worse, to enable them to maintain their desired lifestyles in retirement. They do not know where to turn for help.

- The overwhelming majority have no idea what they are paying in fees, whether the results of their investments have been good or bad, or whether they are on track to achieve their goals.

- Yet more are spending hours every week reading 'hot tips' in the financial pages, picking individual stocks that get them precisely nowhere in the long term.

There has never been a more pressing need for a different approach.

There is a smart way to look after your money

We introduce you to a better way of looking after and growing your money; one that may go against everything you think you know about investment, or at least what the investment business would like you to believe.

Our approach is simple – focusing your energies on things you *can* control – such as saving, spending, costs, taxes and sound financial planning, only taking risks that you know will be rewarded. This places you, the investor, at the centre of the picture, firmly in command of your financial future.

The smart approach to investing your money we outline in this book is not new; it has been very well tested academically in the USA and the UK and is widely used by institutional investors. For individual investors it is a relatively unknown strategy – extremely effective but to date little publicised. There is a good reason for this: the financial services establishment would prefer you not to know about these secrets. They have a vested interest in keeping them quiet to maintain the status quo because they earn far more money out of the old system than the alternative we propose to you here.

Why we decided to write this book

We are four finance professionals with a century of experience between us who have collaborated to provide this clear guide to personal investment success.

We all have a different finance specialism (Ben in wealth management for the over 55s and Richard in wealth management for entrepreneurs, Bruce in life planning and Simon in wealth mentoring), and each of us runs a successful independent advisory firm – we could indeed be seen as competitors in the field of financial advice. Despite our different backgrounds and separate companies we share a common belief – that there is a better way to manage and protect your money. We thought it so important to uncover the hidden truths around money that we decided to pool our expertise.

We came together initially as a study group to research investment ideas and strategies that were starting to work well in the USA and for some large, corporate investors around the world. What we learned has led us to change the way we run our businesses and advise our clients. In order to spread these ideas to as many private investors as possible, we decided to write this book.

At a time of deep financial crisis our most cherished institutions have been found wanting. We know that there is a desperate need for knowledge and confidence to navigate this and future financial storms. We want to give you the inside track so you can make sound financial choices and build a secure financial future for yourself and your family.

It is time we passed the industry's secrets on.

What you will learn from this book

In *The 7 Secrets of Money* we will show you how to cut through the noise, the advertising and the hype to the truth about money. The book will equip you with the knowledge and tools you need to cope and prosper successfully as you develop your financial plans.

You may be surprised to discover that:

- As an individual investor there are powerful forces conspiring against you – the messages communicated by the financial establishment and much of the media are costing you dear (Chapters 1 and 2).

- Markets are efficient to the extent that hardly anyone beats them over time: forecasting is futile and unnecessary (Chapter 3).

- A solid understanding of risk is important if you are going to make informed investment decisions and avoid disaster (Chapter 4).

- Strategic asset allocation – how you distribute the different types of investment in your portfolio – is the most important decision of all (Chapter 5).

- Your behaviour as an investor will define the returns you get (Chapter 6).

Arming you with these revelations and insider knowledge, we give you a clear path to building your investments and meeting your life goals.

You will be relieved to learn that, if you focus on the things you can control, investing is fundamentally a simple process.

- We set out a straightforward methodology for you to follow – *just seven smart actions you need to take to ensure financial success* (Chapter 7 and Conclusion).

Financial planning to meet your life goals

Whatever your financial goals, this book will help you to find a clear way to achieve them. We will help you to make the crucially important connection between your money and your life, stressing the importance of robust financial planning in the context of your life goals.

Our aim is to give you more confidence around finance and investment and a much easier, happier relationship with money.

Who can benefit from reading the book?

There is something for everybody in this book, from the financial novice just starting out and wondering what to do with his/her money to the seasoned investor working hard to get the best return.

■ When you start to make financial plans for your future, the breadth and complexity of the choices you have are so vast that many decide to give up before they have really started. This book will help you navigate a clear path.

■ More sophisticated investors will learn the secrets that by and large only professional investors know. With the information in this book you will be far better informed and able to make better decisions to increase your wealth through investment.

Whatever situation you are in, *The 7 Secrets of Money* will provide the information you need to manage your money intelligently.

The contents will also be valuable for professionals on the edge of money management who are expected to know a lot about it (such as accountants and lawyers); for trustees and particularly professional trustees; for financial journalists who want to improve their understanding; for those trying to decide which adviser to instruct; and for anyone who has become unexpectedly or suddenly wealthy.

How to use this book

Our book is designed to equip you with the information you need to better understand your relationship with money, engage the right adviser and follow the right investment strategy.

The 7 Secrets of Money is not designed as a do-it-yourself finance and investment manual. As you will read in Chapter 6, we strongly believe (perhaps as you might expect) in the need for expert financial guidance to keep you on track along the way.

If you want to get a thorough understanding of the background to the financial world and the actions you need to take, we suggest you read the book from beginning to end. Alternatively, the chapters can be read in isolation if you have an interest in a certain area.

We have tried to present the facts in a manner that is readable and that avoids the somewhat dry nature of the academic research it is based on. For those of you whose interest is awakened, we provide more information and sources in the reading list and notes at the end of the book.

You will find further information, articles and resources on our website, www.7secretsofmoney.co.uk.

It is time to now introduce you to the seven secrets of money and a smarter approach for investment success. Keep an open mind as you read. We are going to shoot down some holy cows and replace them with what you will come to understand as pure common sense.

Apply the alternative approach that we lay out here and see how your relationship with money changes for the better.

Warning: Some of what you read in the following pages will, we hope, challenge beliefs you have held and even make you question some of the financial decisions you have taken in the past.

There is nothing wrong with this: you made those decisions based upon the best information you had available at the time. We made the same mistakes too before we realised that the sources we originally learned from may not have given us the best information or had our best interests at heart.

> *I know that most men, including those
> at ease with problems of the greatest
> complexity, can seldom accept the simplest
> and most obvious truth if it be such as
> would oblige them to admit the falsity
> of conclusions which they have proudly
> taught to others, and which they have
> woven, thread by thread, into the fabric of
> their life.*
>
> Tolstoy[1]

Glossary of terms

Jargon-free definitions of the important financial terms and approaches you will see repeatedly throughout the book.

- *Active investing:* Buying investments to beat the stock market. This strategy is usually based on stock picking, market timing or a combination of both.

- *Asset allocation:* The proportion of your investments you decide to hold in different asset classes – the most crucial decision any investor will take.

- *Asset class:* A group of securities that exhibit similar characteristics, behave similarly in the marketplace, and are subject to the same laws and regulations. The four main asset classes are equities (stocks), fixed-income (bonds), property and cash. Within each asset class there are sub-asset classes which will exhibit different characteristics, such as small companies (small cap) and large companies (large cap), or government-fixed income and corporate-backed fixed income.

- *Bear market:* A stock market in which the prices of shares are falling and expected to continue to fall.

- *Behavioural finance:* The study of the influence of psychology on the behaviour of financial practitioners and investors, and the subsequent effect on markets and investor behaviour.

- *Bonds:* Fixed-income investments. A bond is a loan, usually to a company or government, with a formal contract to repay the borrowed money with interest at fixed intervals.

- **Bull market:** A stock market in which prices are rising and are expected to continue rising.

- **Buy and hold:** Buying investments for the long term and avoiding trading apart from small purchases and sales necessary to bring a portfolio back into balance (see Rebalancing).

- **Diversification:** The process of spreading your investments globally across a number of different types of markets and asset classes.

- **Equity mix:** The type of equities you want to own in your portfolio. This will include the proportion of value stocks and growth stocks to own as well as the size of the companies involved.

- **Gilts:** Bonds issued by a government which might carry less chance of default than a corporate bond.

- **Index fund or Index tracker:** A collective investment scheme that aims to replicate the movements of an index of a specific financial market, or a set of rules of ownership that are held constant, regardless of market conditions.

- **Passive investing:** A 'buy-and-hold' approach to investment, rather than seeking to forecast potential short-term returns.

- **Rebalancing:** The process of buying asset classes which have fallen below their agreed allocations and selling those which have risen above to bring a portfolio back into balance.

- **Smart indexing:** A term coined by the authors of this book to describe our recommended passive approach. This smart approach determines which asset classes are worth holding for the long term, based on academic evidence gathered over the last 50 years. Assets are purchased in the most efficient and diverse manner – without undue trading costs or stock-specific risk – to achieve your desired returns.

SECRET NO.

There is a
financial conspiracy
going on

1.1 Introduction

> Conspiracy: *an evil, unlawful, treacherous or surreptitious plan formulated in secret.*

Conspiracy is a strong word suggesting duplicitous and unpleasant behaviour. We debated long and hard on whether this was too strong a term – should we be more cautious or even-handed? We concluded that conspiracy is exactly the right word for the current state of affairs.

This chapter shows how the financial establishment as a whole conspires against individual investors, transferring significant chunks of wealth to its organisations and reducing your returns. It explains why the financial establishment does not act in your best interests, and gives examples of charges and poor products to look out for.

The industry's aims are not well aligned with the aims of individual investors. In fact, in far too many cases they are completely at odds with your aims. The industry will try to persuade you to purchase the products that make the establishment the most money.

The result for investors? You often pay far too much for over-hyped products with poor returns. Not all products and advisers are bad, but the average net result for individual investors is abysmal.

We mention two studies later in this chapter (section 1.8):

■ One found that between 1989 and 2009 average returns for investors in stocks were 4.25% per annum when average stock market returns were 8.2%. [2]

■ The other found that between 1992 and 2000 investors were receiving 4.91% per annum when markets were delivering 8.99%. [3]

Results that poor warrant words like 'abysmal' and 'conspiracy'.

We hope that this chapter will awaken your inner sceptic and put you one step ahead of the conspirators.

1.2 The conspirators

The financial establishment conspires to transfer as much of your wealth to itself as possible. If this is the motivation, and we believe it is, then this collective aim is entirely at odds with you enjoying a successful and satisfying investment experience.

There are well-documented examples of those who aim to take your money criminally – Bernie Madoff[4] being the most recent and notorious – but this chapter focuses on entirely legal and reputable conspirators.

There are as ever some glorious exceptions, but in general our conspirators include:

1. **Product manufacturers – those who manufacture retail investment products**: life insurance companies, mutual fund companies, banks and others.

2. **Product distributors – those who sell retail investment products**: life insurance companies, mutual fund companies, banks, financial advisers and others.

3. **Those who neither manufacture nor directly encourage you to purchase products or shares but are indirectly financially dependent on your continued purchase of such goods and services**: much of the financial press and ancillary services such as fund rating agencies.

Every penny that you pay to the first two groups is a deduction from your net investment return.

1.3 Why they conspire against us

As we have already stated, we believe that most of the financial industry's aims are counterproductive to your goals as an individual investor:

■ You want to invest wisely and prudently over all time periods in order to achieve your goals while keeping in mind your overall values.

■ The conspirators want to generate the best short-term returns for themselves. Their income increases quickly if they can persuade us investors to be active and to buy and sell lots of products.

Here is an illustration of how this all works. (NB: The company names that follow are all fictitious, but the examples are based on the actions of real companies.)

- As a senior employee at 'FundsAreUs Ltd' your duty is largely to your ***shareholders***, not to your customers. 'FundsAreUs Ltd' and their peers, 'PrivateBankIllusion Ltd' and 'FlavourOfTheMonthAdvisers Ltd', have grown extremely successful and valuable businesses while producing results for clients that vary between OK and shocking. Their interest is in preserving the status quo, in retaining and growing their profitable and cash-generative businesses, not in helping to make our investments grow.

The UK is second only to the USA in terms of the size of its fund management industry. In 2008 the UK fund management industry looked after £3.7 trillion. This increased to £4.1 trillion in 2009.[5] The industry employs 50,000 individuals. These are conservative figures from IFSL (International Financial Services London).[6] The 2008 figure was 12% down on the previous year, but the previous five years saw average annual growth of 8% per annum. This is a huge, successful industry.

The UK fund management industry knows that retail investors are 'sticky'. Once they have signed up as clients the chances of them moving are slim. The same applies to bank accounts: most individual clients (the authors included) cannot be bothered to switch banks very often. While individual clients account for only about 20% of total funds under management, they are far less demanding than institutional clients and individually have no purchasing power with which to negotiate price reductions.

Product manufacturers are strongly motivated to come up with new products that generate ever higher margins for their shareholders. The year 2008/09 will be remembered as the period of the most serious global financial problems since the Great Depression. Following such a period there is huge pressure to rebuild margins and turnover.

1.4 How they take your money

Turnover for fund management companies comes not just from annual management charges but from anything that the consumer pays, such as:

1. ***Dealing commissions.*** Every time a fund manager deals in a security there is a charge or commission. This is borne by the end client. Therefore the more activity taking place within a fund, the higher the revenue for the fund management house, broker or other party.

The key point to remember is that when stocks are bought or sold, someone gets paid; and that *someone* is paid by you, the individual investor. This increased revenue does not depend on winning new clients – the existing clients pay out and do not have to authorise such payments.

This situation leads to an incentive for someone to be *'active'*.[7] The more active a fund manager or discretionary manager is, the higher the revenue for *someone* per client and per £1 of assets under management.

Active fund management is a complex area. A fund manager, or a fund manager's firm, may not benefit in any direct way from activity; but rest assured that some party or other does. As you will read in Chapter 3, there is clear evidence that higher activity does not result in better results for the client – in fact on average it damages results for the client. No one in the financial establishment wants you to know this, so a huge effort is made to justify all this activity.

Fund managers and brokers publish sheets explaining why they have sold X and bought Y; they run seminars, put broadcasts up on the web and communicate in any low-cost way they can come up with to let you know how their informed, professional activity is the best thing for you. Such activity can be very reassuring during times of difficulty – it feels right that your manager/broker is working day and night to seek out the latest and best investment opportunities for you; he is not just sitting tight while Rome burns.

But look for the evidence. If there is compelling evidence that lots of activity can generate better returns than limited activity, then this evidence would surely be very useful for the fund management industry.

For the authors of this book, the debate is over. There is a wealth of compelling, rigorous academic evidence that in fact ***activity usually reduces the net return for clients***. The fund management industry as a whole is not exactly crazy about publicising this evidence but there is plenty of it available (see Chapter 3).

(NB: You will find references to studies throughout the following chapters and in the notes section of the book.[8] This research is carried out by highly respected organisations: it is peer reviewed and authored by notable professors around the world. Some of the authors of this research advise the largest institutional investors; others are Nobel Laureate winners.)

How else do they make you pay?

2. ***Other fees***. Commissions are not the only fees taken by the industry (or 'the croupier', as John Bogle, author and founder of investment management company The Vanguard Group,[9] refers to it). Do not forget depositary fees, custody fees, valuation fees, accountancy including audit fees, bid-offer spreads and so on.

An FSA Occasional Paper looked at the fees involved in retail funds.[10] Specifically it looked at the costs incurred when a fund decided to sell one share and buy another. The paper concluded that the average cost of selling Share X and buying Share Y (often known as a 'round trip') in the UK was estimated at 1.8%. This means that if a fund manager or broker decides to sell £10,000 of Stock X and use the proceeds to buy Stock Y, when the transactions are complete the fund will have only £9,820 invested. This number (1.8%) varies a lot depending on the underlying security and the market on which it is being traded. A major contributory factor in the UK is stamp duty.

There are several reports available that look at the total fees incurred by funds when they trade and also at how often the fund trades. This frequency of trading is known as 'stock turnover'. The more the fund trades, the more the cost of trading rises. In the end it is the investor who pays all these costs. Popular funds often have turnover of 100%. A rate of 200% is not unusual. 100% turnover means that on average every holding in the fund is changed once per annum.

This is a huge cost. Imagine a fund with an annual fee of 1.0% – that is still considered pretty reasonable in the UK – and a portfolio turnover of 150%. This means that the total costs of the fund are 1.0% + (150% x 1.8%) = 3.7% per annum.

3.7% per annum![11] That is a big number!

So the industry's aims (increased turnover, increased profits, increased turnover per account, increased profit per account) are entirely in opposition to your aims. The industry (in which we include brokers, dealers, fund managers, insurance companies, registrars, custodians et al.) does not want you to know this, hence our use of the word 'conspiracy'.

But even that is not the whole story. The consumer continues to pay:

3. *Sales charges.* There are also a whole host of sales charges that can be added when the entity selling the investment persuades a retail investor to buy. The UK retail industry still endures something known as 'bid-offer' spreads. The bid-offer spread is the difference in price of an investment depending on whether you are buying or selling.

The UK fund management industry often charges a bid-offer spread that does not reflect the spread of the underlying assets. It is common to pay 5% as an entry cost to a product in the UK.

If all this seems a little too full of jargon, another way of thinking of it is as follows: if you put £100 on deposit in your bank at 12.01 p.m. on Monday, you would expect that at 12.02 it would still be worth £100. But if you invest £100 in a typical unit trust in the UK at 12.01 p.m. on Monday, by 12.02 the investment will be worth about £95.

The vendors of these products will of course justify these sales costs. They will refer to them as 'distribution' costs. Whatever the label is, it is a cost that you are suffering and you should know about it.

We have been writing articles for years about these costs – which are basically commissions for the vendor. Over this time the industry has found better and better ways of obscuring the true level of these charges. It is still perfectly possible to receive commission of 7% for selling clients particular products, and this is over and above the annual management charges that we have already mentioned!

NOTE: This book was written prior to new legislation in the UK that effectively outlaws commission payments for independent advisers. Please see the addendum on page 175 for a little more information on this legislation.

Question your bank's advice

The conspirators here are not the hapless trainee advisers at 'PrivateBankIllusion Ltd' – they are the most senior management at 'GlobalBank plc', which owns 'PrivateBankIllusion Ltd'.

They devise complex and carefully structured training courses for their staff to teach them that the distribution costs are remarkably competitive. The staff are also told that they will earn no commission on the sale of these products. They do, however, (in at least one high-street bank) earn 'points'. Different contracts earn different numbers of points. And at the end of the year or quarter the adviser's bonus will not be unrelated to the number of points he has 'earned'.

Advisers are placed under great pressure to deliver the bank's high-margin products (which carry high points value) in preference to lower-margin products; while at the same time the advisers will be told to sell only the product that is most suitable for their clients. This trite caveat will be used as evidence by the banks that they advise clients only to buy the most suitable product. Or the least unsuitable. Or something.

1.5 Beware of structured products – just too good to be true

There is room here for a special mention for *structured products*, specifically bank-sponsored structured products. Structured products are the 'heads you win, tails you don't lose' products that have become very popular in the last few years. Typical arrangements will be:

- Invest £100,000 for four years. If the FTSE and the DAX rise over the four-year period your investment return will be the equivalent of 120% of the average capital return of the FTSE and the DAX over the four-year period. If after four years the FTSE and DAX have lost money then you will lose no money and your £100,000 will be returned.

Structured products look a bit like an each-way bet that you cannot lose (or, as one of the authors of this book describes it, the financial services equivalent of a delicious chocolate cake served with double cream and only five calories a portion!).

While the proposal may appear superficially attractive, it is essential to dig in to the detail and establish exactly what is being offered. In many, many cases the return you can reasonably expect from such offers is substantially less than you might reasonably expect to achieve from an equity investment. In most though not all cases the high street bank will deliver what it promises; what smart investors must do is examine the promise in detail.

Take the arrangement outlined above: the dividends alone over four years might amount to around 14%. The average value of an index is always much lower than the highest value. Most importantly you are taking out what appears to be a diversified investment when typically you are reliant on a third party (often unknown) to pay out the return. This proved costly where the counterparty was Lehman Brothers! (See box on following page.)

In the context of structured products it is entirely reasonable to compare the high street bank with a croupier. Casinos do generally pay the promised odds. Some individuals can win large amounts of money at casinos. But on average, gamblers at casinos lose and what really takes place is a transfer of wealth from gambler to croupier. The odds are in their favour. The casinos do not exist to help their clients.

Our client banks are made up exclusively of fantastic people with whom we truly enjoy dealing. They are wealthy and bright. And still we get questions from them about the latest structured product from 'PrivateBankIllusion Ltd', something of which we would expect rational people to steer well clear.

Stop and consider these points

Investments that look too good to be true are pretty much without exception exactly that. Before you jump to take a bite of that apple, step back and ask two questions. The first is:

1. ***What are the fees?*** All fees are deductions from your total

Lehman Brothers

Lehman Brothers was a famous investment bank with a proud history stretching back to the mid 19th century. By the 21st century they were one of the largest investment banks in the world. In late 2008 Lehman Brothers Holding Inc. filed for bankruptcy. Amongst Lehmans' many activities, one was to back structured products available to UK (and American) investors. Lehmans' bankruptcy caused serious problems for UK investors. Some structured products purchased by UK investors did not pay out as promised: not because of a market collapse, but because of the failure of one bank.

To give an example, NDF was a well-known manufacturer of structured product targeted at the UK consumer market. Lehman Brothers backed some of the products it sold. When Lehman Brothers failed, consumers did not receive the returns promised by the product literature and NDF.

With the benefit of hindsight it is easy to question the wisdom of investing in a product entirely dependent on just one large bank, but we must remember that:

■ Many investors had no idea that Lehmans was the supplying bank (or 'counterparty'). They had no direct contractual arrangement with Lehmans. In much NDF literature there was no mention of Lehman Brothers at all.

■ The marketing was compelling. The plans backed by Lehmans had names like 'Capital Secure Fixed Growth Plan'. They used words such as '100% capital secure'.

■ Sophisticated, financially savvy investors bought this product, and sophisticated and apparently financially savvy advisers recommended it.

Structured products are still being marketed at the time of writing with the backing of one or a small number of investment banks. It is pretty much impossible to eliminate all risks. The trick is to have as complete an understanding of the risks you are taking as possible. (See Secret 4 of this book.)

return, so it seems fair to ask what they are.

Most advisers seem remarkably vague on this point. The most common (verbal) answer is that there are no fees – no annual management costs, no bid-offer spreads. Since 'PrivateBankIllusion Ltd' has not morphed into a registered charity, this is plainly utter poppycock.

A glance or scour through the documentation might reveal typical fees of 10%, but it is hard to find out what the true number actually is. This is because of the way products like this are designed.

There are several variations, but the basic design is that 'PrivateBankIllusion Ltd' and 'GlobalBank plc' telephone an investment bank and ask them what it would cost for the investment bank to offer 'PrivateBankIllusion Ltd' returns such as the average of the DAX/FTSE return over a four-year period and a money-back guarantee. The investment bank gives them an answer. (NB: Do not rule out the possibility that 'GlobalBank plc' might own the investment bank.) 'PrivateBankIllusion Ltd' then just adds its margin and sells the product to clients like you. A simple wholesale/retail mark-up.

But of course the investment bank has added its margin into the price offered to 'PrivateBankIllusion Ltd'. How does the investment bank reduce its risk? It reduces it by a complicated pattern of holding mixtures of stock, cash and options. The stocks all have to be bought (more fees for you) and all the options have to be purchased (yet more fees). More complicated structures involve 'GlobalBank plc' retaining some money on deposit or purchasing some of the protection.

There are a huge number of parties making money out of these structured products, and this is normally a surefire sign for rational investors to keep well away. These parties with their opaque fees are conspirators: keep an eye on your wallet.

The second question to ask is:

2. **Is this alchemy?** Structured products seem to remove a great deal of the risk but still offer stock-market-type returns. Investors should be healthily sceptical about such claims.

It is important to remember that ***risk and return are related: if risk is reduced then expected returns are reduced*** (you will learn more about this in Chapter 4). If in the very long term cash produces an expected return of inflation + 1%, and equities (the stock market) produce an expected return of inflation + 5%, then strategies which have less risk than a typical equity portfolio will have an expected return of less than inflation + 5%.

So if the fees are substantial (as they invariably are with structured products from high-street banks), then in many cases the expected return is going to start getting very close to that of cash or fixed interest, no matter how compelling the brochure.

In our opinion structured products rarely make sense for clients – they are nothing but overpriced, opaque and illiquid high-street bank products.

We leave you with a warning: ***investments that are complicated, tough to analyse and appear too good to be true are dangerous.*** Tread with great care.

1.6 Beware of statistics from product distributors

The conspirators stand to make huge amounts of money if they can convince retail investors to buy their product. The senior staff's bonuses and the value of their share options depend upon persuading you to buy their product. Clever use of fund performance statistics is one of their most persuasive tools.

Product distributors will shamelessly ignore all their actively managed funds that have underperformed the market and will spend huge amounts of money advertising the small number of funds that have performed well.

The industry has been attempting to convince clients to buy on the back of fund performance for as long as we have been in the industry. Consider this example:

- A fund that loses 5% a year for four years and makes 50% in year five has average fund performance of about 4% a year.

- But a fund advertised as showing returns of 4% per annum over the last five years is far more attractive than a fund that has lost money in four out of the last five years.

This example might appear silly, and we might reassure ourselves that we would not fall for something so obviously contrived, but it is an easy trap to fall into. We advise you and advise ourselves to be cautious of all statistics and very cautious of all statistics in marketing: establish the source; check using two or three authoritative sources.

Product distributors' aims are, like the product manufacturers' aims, completely at odds with your aims. Product distributors will try to persuade you to purchase the products that make them the most money.

1.7 The final conspirators – the financial press and ancillary services

So far in this chapter we have sought to run through some examples of those who conspire to part you from your wealth while at the same time half-promising to enhance your wealth. These conspirators will increase their own profitability at your expense.

The final group to mention, and we emphasise again that there are glorious exceptions, is different from the product manufacturers and distributors. This group will not profit from your losses. They are nonetheless beneficiaries of the status quo. This group includes those who are ***indirectly financially dependent on your continued purchase of such goods and services*** – much of the financial press and the ancillary services such as credit rating agencies.

Those who comment on personal finance in journals are incessantly schmoozed by the insurance companies, fund managers, banks and brokers – you will read more about these in the next chapter. Most publications (dailies, weeklies and monthlies) are commercially dependent on advertising from these organisations. Without the advertising the publications would not exist. This exerts pressure on journalists not to be frightfully rude about those who are ultimately paying them. It would be a brave journalist who wrote in scathing general terms about their ultimate paymaster. So criticism tends to be far more specific – articles about index huggers, poorly performing endowments or administration failings are commonplace. Far rarer are broadside attacks on the industry. This lends weight to our belief in a conspiracy.

There is another difficulty for journalists. The authors of this volume believe that for most of our private clients, investment should be fairly boring. Investors should acknowledge that the market is broadly efficient and stop wasting time and money trying to beat it in any conventional sense (see Chapter 3). Clients should instead concentrate on achieving all that is important to them while keeping a close eye on fees and taxes (we cover this in Chapter 7). If at a fundamental level this is all there is to investment, then there is arguably much less for journalists to write about!

1.8 Invest with your eyes wide open

When you embark on investment, remember that most of those who manufacture product, those who distribute product and those on the fringes of those two fundamental positions are not necessarily working in your interests and would all rather like the current arrangements to continue. They get extraordinarily wealthy by convincing you that you need their services and that they will give you an advantage over other, less exciting but rather less expensive options.

- Consider a typical 60-year-old investor with a £1,000,000 portfolio. It is so well invested that it generates a regular annual return of 8% per annum. Total fees, commissions and other leakage amount to about 3% per annum. After just ten years the investor's portfolio will be worth between £1,500,000 and £1,600,000, depending on the detail of the deductions.

- Now consider the conspirators' position. They withdraw 3% per annum and manage to invest it at 8% and suffer no leakage. After the same ten years from a standing start they now have between £500,000 and £600,000. So the 60-year-old investor, who probably worked for much of his life to get the £1,000,000, gets about half the benefits of the investment return and the croupier takes the other half.

We appreciate that this example is crude but *is it any surprise that the croupier and his staff want to maintain the status quo?*

- Most investors would be happy if, starting out with £1,000,000 at the age of 60, the industry offered a likely return of 8% per annum before charges; if instead they were offered £1,200,000 growth over ten years in exchange for a fee of £500,000, we suspect there would be some heavy negotiation.

We close with a few more statistics to show the effect of the conspiracy.

The latest study from American research company Dalbar[12] (dated April 2013 and covering data from January 1993 to December 2012) concludes that over the previous 20 years:

- The average equity investor received 4.25% per annum;
- Inflation was 2.4%;
- Yet the S&P 500 returned 8.2%!

In his thesis in 2007, author Lukas Schneider looked at UK data.[13] He concluded that between 1992 and 2000:

- The average annual return on stocks was 8.99%.
- The average fund offered a return of 6.93% per annum.
- The average fund investor received a return of 4.91% per annum. (NB: Inflation over the period was 2.5% per annum.)

The arguments as to why it is so difficult to beat the market are based in financial theory but have very important real-world implications. The difference in the above studies between the market return and the return received by investors is huge. *No wonder most individual investors are unhappy with the returns on their portfolio!*

We believe the difference can be explained by two key points.

1. *The fees charged by the industry are high.* Most retail funds are in actively managed funds where fees are higher than in passive funds (you will find out more about this in Chapter 3).

2. *Retail investors time their decisions to invest and to switch appallingly.* When performance in a sector takes off there are a huge number of fund launches (the conspirators all meet and rub their hands in joy) and money flows in, and very often the sector then suffers a correction or a collapse. Retail investors stay around for a little while but eventually sell (to fund the purchase of the next new thing), and soon after they have sold, the sector that had collapsed starts to recover. Meanwhile their experience in the first fund is now repeated in the more recent purchase.

You are the clients with the liquid assets – we are just advisers. Stock markets exist not to make you or anybody else rich. They exist a) to bring businesses that need capital together with those that have capital; and b) to facilitate the buying and selling of stocks.

You, as a provider of capital, are entitled to a return on that capital that reflects the risks of that provision of capital. Do not let the conspirators take so much of the return as to make the whole exercise pointless.

1.9 Conclusion

This chapter has outlined some of the main players in the financial services industry. We have attempted to explain what motivates them and why this motivation means that your interests are poorly aligned with theirs.

They are not evil: they are merely behaving in a largely economically rational way. There are also exceptions. There are fabulous investment companies, superb bank advisers and many brilliant journalists. The key point to remember is that their financial success is not in any direct short- or medium-term way linked to your financial success. The current status quo has made many companies and their shareholders wealthy. While there is a growing questioning of these institutions and their dealings with the public, these organisations are strongly incentivised to perpetuate the current arrangements.

In the next chapter we will look at some of the material that is distributed to persuade you that 'FundsAreUs' and 'PrivateBankIllusion' really are the best organisations to guide you through the investment minefield.

SECRET NO.

The financial press peddles *investment pornography*

2.1 Introduction

Achieve better results than
the market by following our tips

Shrewd investors fix
rates as interest rates
head for decline

The six best shares
for the next 12 months

Five top tips for stellar investments

Huge volumes of verbiage are produced each day
about investment. This chapter urges you to be highly
sceptical about what you read in the financial media.

We strongly believe that the personal finance pages, the weekly investment magazines, the monthly magazines and tip sheets that many investors love to read, peddle advice that is, in the main, little more than investment porn. It is designed to excite, but ultimately it is really not very good for you.

Slavishly following this type of advice is expensive; the predictions will fail you again and again. We know from experience that reading and studying this type of information acts as a barrier to taking considered and informed financial action.

This chapter is designed to open your eyes to the titillating, addictive nature of the financial press. We implore you to wean yourself off it as a first influencer for your financial decisions.

2.2 The financial media: a source of good tips or titillating pornography?

Conventional pornography is widely available. Most readers of this book will be aware of how to recognise it and of the downsides that can result from overexposure. The investment industry has its own pornography. It is widely available and no less titillating.

Investment pornography is very similar to conventional pornography; indeed, it differs only in one significant way: involvement in the production and consumption of investment pornography is socially acceptable.

There are similarities between investment and traditional pornography:

- Both are big business.
- Both can be addictive.
- Producers of both have a vested interest in persuading you that that their material is harmless.
- Both are designed to excite.

The rest of this chapter explores why this type of material is so prevalent in the financial industry. We hope to demonstrate what a damaging influence it can have on your investment decisions. When you can recognise this material for what it really is you will be far more likely to shrug your shoulders, turn the page and look for better sources of information.

Once you have read this chapter, thumb through your broadsheet at the weekend: glance at how many advertisements (or advertorials) are funded by the investment industry. You might be surprised by what you see.

2.3 The financial press can mislead gullible consumers

If the only education individuals received on how to build and maintain rewarding relationships was via top-shelf magazines combined with the instructional videos available on the internet, then these individuals' ability to build and maintain such relationships would be pretty limited. In the world of investment many people base their decisions on advice that is equally unhelpful.

Consider statements we have read in the financial media recently such as:

There is no reason for the market to be so low

The market should not have reacted like that

You cannot blame the market for an investment decision that fails! Such statements are arrant nonsense.

The stock market is merely the coming together of buyers and sellers. It does not have a personality, or aims, or responsibilities, or feelings. It is merely the aggregate result of institutions and individuals buying or selling shares.

To blame the market for an investment's performance is akin to blaming a thermometer for an illness – it is at best a very sloppy explanation.

The market's level is a function of the transactions entered into recently. The very reason the market is at any particular level is because there have been transactions between others that have priced investments using whatever reasoning was available to the market participators.

Yet investors, when they see a hot tip fail, will blame the market again and again. The market is what it is – it does not need a reason. By volume, the total number of stocks bought is always the same as the total number of stocks sold.

As investors we need to face the fact that we are probably just average performers with good days and bad days. You may hope that if you follow the secret or elite techniques that you have read about in the media you will produce hugely satisfying results. Sadly the evidence is all against you.

If there is a 'guru' out there who can identify which stocks or markets are going to rise in advance of this happening, then why would he or she wish to share this information? The sharing of the information with consumers has an absolutely direct negative impact on the information's value. Surely the shrewd guru would keep the information very close to his chest until he acted upon it? Perhaps he would set up a very tightly controlled investment club which charged huge fees for membership. The manager would not declare how money was invested until after it was invested for fear of devaluing the information. As well as the membership fee this guru could also charge a performance fee.

These clubs actually exist and are called **hedge funds** (more information on hedge funds can be found on our website, www.7secretsofmoney.co.uk). The top hedge funds do not publish their tips on the internet, in the *Mail on Sunday* or the *Sunday Times*.

A poor investment for nearly all investors hedge funds may be, but pornography they are not.

Those funds that publish their tips freely or cheaply are, in the main, peddling porn.

2.4 Financial pornography is addictive

Reading financial columns can be extremely addictive. There is so much commentary produced by so many apparently well-informed sources that readers start to believe that if they read enough of it and act on the recommendations then they too will enjoy excellent results.

Of course, there is a lot of excellent writing on investments. The good stuff, however, is not as a rule immediately exciting. But weekly, daily, even hourly updates seem to be so very relevant that they are at a shallow level far more interesting than great treatises written over months or years by well-qualified experts.

Look again at the statistics we referred to in the last chapter, showing the abysmal returns that individual investors get on average. In the Dalbar survey[1] (see page 27) we saw that investors achieved only 4.25% when the market was returning 8.2%!

The causes of these poor returns are, of course, debatable, but we would submit that the fact that many investors base their investment decisions on what they read in the financial press has a significant impact.

They have read column after column. Each one is slightly different from the one that preceded it, but the basic message is clear:

Achieve better results than the market by following our tips

Sadly the strong mathematical likelihood is that following the tips will actually *reduce* your net returns.

Examples of soft-core headlines

Shrewd investors rush to fix rates as interest rates head for decline

Ten funds to help you profit from the property boom

Which funds are the experts tipping to beat the recession?

Hard-core examples

The ten shares set to outperform this year

The six best shares for the next twelve months

Investors read these predictions and see them fail in real life again and again, yet they cannot wean themselves off the reading material. Where the scientist sees clears evidence and a conclusion, the addict sees failed science and continues to believe the glossy brochures.

The habit can be horribly expensive and terribly time-consuming – the addict truly believes that if only he could read enough tip sheets, then he would be informed enough to win.

2.5 Producers have a vested interest in persuading you that that their material is good for you

The financial media are on to a good thing and want you to believe that their material is beneficial.

Apparently respectable businesses – highly respected businesses at that – are intimately involved in the investment pornography business. It is too lucrative to turn down.

There is a huge marketing function funded by the investment industry. Advertisements for investment funds can change people's behaviour. Senior managers are measured on how much money they are looking after. They are strongly motivated to increase this number. They therefore direct huge marketing spending at:

a. Advertisements that paint their investments in a good light; and

b. Fund launches that encourage investors to invest money in the latest, shiniest fund.

Regulations have been tightened in recent years, and there are many rules that govern the content of investment advertisements. These rules are designed by humans; other humans then try to find ways around the rules or to bend them.

For instance, there are several ways to report fund performance.

Consider a fund with the following results (we will call it the 'Super Duper Fund'[2]):

Figure 1 *Table illustrating the performance of the*
'Super Duper Fund'

Year	Total invested	Annual return	Fund value at year end
1	£10m	20%	£12m
2	£16m	25%	£35m
3	£45m	5%	£84m
4	£36m	–15%	£102m
5	£15m	5%	£122.85m

All the following statements are true, based on this illustration:

■ The 'Super Duper Fund' has produced an average annual return of over 8% since launch (a simple average of the returns).

■ The 'Super Duper Fund' was worth just over £10m five years ago; it is now worth over £120m.

■ The 'Super Duper Fund' has shown positive returns over four out of the last five years.

But the following statements are also true:

■ The 'Super Duper Fund' has attracted £122m in investments over the last five years. It is now worth less than £123m.

■ The 'Super Duper Fund' has produced an average annual return of 0.25% per annum (compound return based on funds invested).

■ Two-thirds of investors in the 'Super Duper Fund' have lost money (if they all invested an equal amount).[3]

The first three statements can be used to paint a very flattering picture of a fund's performance. But they are a distraction. Reading and studying this information acts as a barrier to taking considered, informed action.

2.6 The financial media can titillate and is often sensational

It can be amusing to glance at this material. The scale of the errors is sometimes astonishing. A well-known national mainstream newspaper published the following two headlines:

House prices set to fall further

and ...

House price rises are now likely

They published both these headlines on the same day!

There are hosts of these examples. Here is another good one from a well-known business magazine back in 2001:

Stick with storage ... long term, this simple fact is true: a company can postpone buying new PCs or upgrading its network, but it can't stop producing digital data. The stuff must be put somewhere, and it increasingly gets stored in many places ... Buy EMC Corp. at $44 per share.

*Amazon.com is the exact opposite [of eBay]; it faces –
and has yet to solve – all the problems of offline retailers.
Sell Amazon at $12 per share.*

EMC shares closed at $17.34 on 18 December 2009, down 60%,
while Amazon shares closed at $128.48, up 907%.

It is easy to giggle now with the benefit of hindsight, but when
such statements are carried by respected publications they carry
with them a distinctly non-pornographic air: they seem to be
written with consideration and care.

They may well have been written with consideration and care but,
as you can see, they are of little practical use to most individuals.

2.7 Conclusion – stay sceptical

In the UK there is the Press Complaints Commission,[4] which
is meant to keep journalists in check. But this chapter is about
more than just journalists (and indeed, there are many excellent
financial journalists that we recommend to our clients – no, they
do not all agree with our view, but they are well informed and
interesting).

As we have attempted to illustrate, there are a large number of
powerful organisations involved in the investment pornography
business – we include:

- Nearly all those who design past-performance advertisements.

- Those who try to get advisers to use their fund manager
du jour.

- Those who produce fund directories supported by
advertising budgets.

- Those who rate funds and produce Best Buy lists.

- Those who publish magazines targeting the advisory community with lists of top picks.

It is a big pool. All the people drinking from it are paid by you, the investor. But you do not pay any of them directly.

Bear in mind that investment pornography is at best titillating. It can easily become sinister and damaging. ***If you have a habit, try to wean yourself off it.***

Nearly the last word in this chapter goes to an article from the well-known American publication *Fortune*, published back in April 1999. In a piece entitled 'Confessions of a former mutual funds reporter',[5] the (anonymous) author writes:

> *We [Fortune] were preaching buy-and-hold[6] marriage while implicitly endorsing hot-fund promiscuity … Unfortunately, rational, pro-index-fund stories don't sell magazines, cause hits on websites, or boost Nielsen ratings.*

These words are the truth. Investment pornography is all-pervasive and socially acceptable. The bulk of what we are able to read in periodicals, on the internet and elsewhere is nothing more than pornography. Relying on this as your only source of information and advice leads to dysfunctional behaviour and an unrewarding long-term relationship with money.

Stay sceptical

One of the most common subjects you will read about in the financial press is how to beat the market. The next chapter looks at this important topic, where received wisdom seems to have been greatly influenced by the investment industry's copy.

SECRET NO.

3

You cannot beat
the market

3.1 Introduction

What is really quite remarkable in the investment world is that people are playing a game which, in some sense, cannot be played.

There are so many people out there in the market; the idea that any single individual without extra information or extra market power can beat the market is extraordinarily unlikely. Yet the market is full of people who think they can do it and full of other people who believe them.

This is one of the great mysteries of finance: why do people believe they can do the impossible?

And why do others believe them?

Daniel Kahneman, Professor of Psychology
and Public Affairs, Princeton University,
and 2002 Nobel Prize winner[1]

This chapter exposes one of the key myths about investment management: that through 'canny' stock picking and market timing it is possible to beat the returns offered by the market.

The premise of a huge amount of the investment pornography put about by the financial media is:

Pass your money to me or my firm; we can do better than most. We have superior analysis, superior information, superior stock-picking skills or some other attribute and we will produce over time a better return than the market.

This argument is wrapped and spun in different ways but the fact remains that it is a myth.

In this chapter we suggest that:

1. *It is extremely unlikely that you or anyone else will be able to consistently beat* (in any conventional sense) *the return offered by the market.* Indeed, it is an expensive folly to devote time and money to trying to beat the market. That is why the experts largely do not bother trying.

2. *You do not need to beat the market.* Just by producing market returns you will outstrip most funds and most of your peers over the medium and long term.

3. *There is a more intelligent way to manage your money* that acknowledges 1) and 2) above and is better than buying index funds.

3.2 Why this chapter is so important

The private investor in the UK is besieged with information and quasi-information that is based on the following ideas:

■ Clever managers move in and out of rising and falling markets to get the best return for their clients. Only mugs buy index funds.

■ Large or specialist firms or perhaps very clever people have some advantage because of their research function or their intelligence which enables them to produce returns superior to the market return.

These are the arguments behind the traditional 'active' approach to investment. Have a look at the finance section of your weekend paper: most of the advertisements will be a reworking of one of these two beliefs.

This is a key point: academically there is scant evidence to support the basic propositions above. There are container-loads of academic evidence that cast doubt on the basic propositions of the active/ traditional manager (as you will see in section 3.3).

Even if this weight of academic evidence against an active approach does not put you off, how about this?

- Large, specialist firms and very clever people are expensive resources. It is a lot cheaper not to pay them; and if you do not pay them your returns will probably rise.

3.3 Why it is so unlikely that you can beat the market in the medium or long term

Active management does not stack up when it comes to empirical evidence; it also stands on shaky theoretical ground.

The theory

The market as a whole prices stocks fairly efficiently. If more people think a stock is going to rise than think it is going to fall, then the market will realise this. Almost instantly the stock price will rise to the point where an equal number of market participants think the stock is going to rise as think it will fall.

How does this happen? Because those who think the price is going to fall will sell to those who think it will rise; they will realise that they can ask a little more than the current price and increase their asking price and so on.

This happens remarkably quickly in the 21st century. Huge banks of computers are dedicated to helping sellers to increase prices and helping buyers to reduce prices.

(This is a rough-and-ready explanation of the Efficient Market Hypothesis, or EMH. EMH is in fact a highly refined model and there are several different versions of it. You will find more information on this in the notes at the end of the book.[2])

The evidence

Study after study shows that over significant time periods (say ten years or more) traditional active management has delivered far less than the market return in the vast majority of cases.

There are so many studies that it is tough to decide which ones to quote, but here are a few:

- In 1993, in the first major study of bond market performance, looking at US Mutual funds, financial economists Christopher Blake, Edwin J. Elton and Martin J. Gruber examined 361 bond funds for the period starting in 1977.[3] They compared the various active funds to simple index strategy alternatives. The authors found that the active funds, on average, underperform the index strategies by 0.85% a year. Depending on the benchmark, 65 to 80% of the funds underperformed the benchmark.

- In a 1993 study of equity mutual funds, Elton and Gruber joined forces with two other economists, Matthew Hlavka and Sanjiv Das, to examine all funds that existed for the period 1965–84;[4] 143 funds in all. These funds are compared to the set of index funds – big stocks, small stocks and fixed income – that most closely correspond to the actual investment choices made by the mutual funds. The result: on average these funds underperform the index funds by a whopping 1.59%

a year! Not a single fund generated positive performance that was statistically significant.

- A 2008 study[5] by Laurent Barras, Oliver Scaillet and Russel L. Wermers published by the Swiss Finance Institute shows that only one in 166 managers actually demonstrates any skill in relation to the market.

- Jensen[6] in the 1960s produced compelling data that suggested that manager fees rather than manager skill was the biggest determinant of performance.

- Mark Carhart,[7] who became head of quantitative analysis at Goldman Sachs, looked at twenty years' worth of data. He came to broadly similar conclusions.

(If you would like more evidence please do drop us an email.)

Many of the relevant analyses look to establish how much of a manager's return is due to luck (good or bad) and how much is due to something else.

If we accept the Efficient Market Hypothesis we would certainly expect to find managers who perform better than the market from time to time. We would also expect to find those who underperform from time to time. It is only useful to an investor to know who is likely to outperform if he knows that information in advance of the outperformance. Sadly manager performance to date has almost no predictive power in respect of future manager performance (apart from the fact that bad managers usually stay that way).

Figure 2 helps to illustrate this.

Figure 2 *The distribution of actual returns of 1,302 managers, 1962–95*[8]

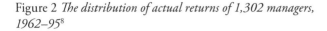

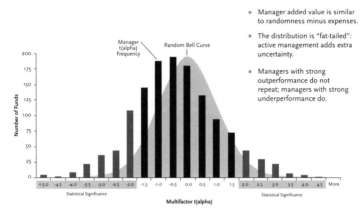

- Manager added value is similar to randomness minus expenses.

- The distribution is "fat-tailed": active management adds extra uncertainty.

- Managers with strong outperformance do not repeat; managers with strong underperformance do.

Source: Mark Carhart, "On Persistence in Mutual Fund Performance," Journal of Finance, 52, no.1 (March 1997)   Distribution of Multifactor t(alpha) 1,302 Managers 1962-1995

■ The thick blocks are the actual results of fund managers over a 33-year period.

■ The grey curvy bit shows the returns we might expect if managers just picked their stocks randomly – by chance.

You will notice that the two results look pretty similar – the managers' results look not unlike the random results *except* that the managers' results are a bit to the left of the random results. This is probably because managers have quite high fees. These fees mean that on average managers perform worse than a random selection. (Before we are inundated with letters and emails from technically savvy managers, yes, we know something about fat tails and kurtosis and all that jazz – it does not detract from the basic point.)

Grasping this idea is not a pleasant experience. Throwing darts at the *FT* will produce returns that are comparable with professional managers' returns; factor in fees and you are better off with the darts, depending on what you charge for dart throwing.

We prescribe a smart investment strategy based on scientific inquiry in the field of finance rather than on anecdotal evidence. The tests have been done and they are well documented. Unfortunately for many investors, the subject of these tests has been not lab rats but real people with real money!

3.4 Summing up – the final nails in the coffin for active management

An active manager has only two arrows in his quiver – market timing and stock picking. All nuanced forms of active management ultimately boil down to some combination of these two elements. Both fundamentally rely on predicting the future, and the information presented in support of the forecast is typically quite compelling.

Statements are made such as 'we think the price of oil will rise because …' or 'we think the economy will recover next year because …' .

No matter how convincing the case may seem, however, you should always ask why this information, which is readily available to the market, would not already be reflected in prices.

Active managers argue that they can gather information and gain insight or knowledge through superior research into a company, to beat the market. This is not necessarily the case; you and I could have a different set of information or a different interpretation of the same information, while other investors may have no information at all. Neither of us, however, is at an advantage or disadvantage because the aggregate of all information is already contained in prices. So, rather than gaining insight or knowledge, the manager is simply gathering information the market has already digested.

The Efficient Market Hypothesis we mention suggests that current market prices are the best estimate of fair value based upon available information. This is not to say that prices are always correct. The market may get prices wrong from time to time – some prices are too high and others are too low – but it does so randomly and unpredictably.

No investor can systematically outperform other investors, or the market as a whole. The fact that prices can change dramatically is not a sign of market inefficiency. It is a reflection of how quickly prices can adjust to a new equilibrium based on the latest information or news which, by definition, is new.

There is a dilemma facing active investors who believe that pricing errors are identifiable for profit at the expense of someone else. If the price is wrong today, how can one be sure the market will eventually arrive at the 'correct' price in the future? Is the market inefficient today but efficient tomorrow, or is there a chance an investor will go to his grave as the only one who knows the right price?

There is good data covering at least the last 50-year history of professional investment management. The message is clear: *the beat-the-market efforts of professionals are impressively and overwhelmingly negative.* In any asset class, the only consistently superior performer is the market itself.

3.5 The passive alternative – an altogether smarter approach

- *Active managers* seek to forecast potential short-term movements in prices of assets or entire markets.

- *Passive investment* recognises that markets are broadly efficient and difficult to beat.

Passive (or enhanced passive) managers acknowledge that, in aggregate, the performance of all the participants in the market *is* the market. It is intellectually illiterate to think that for most of the time the majority of the active managers can outperform the market. In fact, when either the theory or the evidence is examined, active managers produce a net return that is markedly less than the market return.

Shrewd investors, particularly those charged with an obligation to be prudent, give up chasing the elusive active manager because this is a high-risk strategy. Instead they patiently decide on which asset classes to own, and then own them in a highly diversified index-type fund or structure. This hugely reduces activity (so lowers costs) and avoids the risk of owning the wrong stocks (resulting in less underperformance) and so leads to performance that over time is greatly superior to a typical actively managed fund.

William Sharpe – professor of finance and Nobel Prize winner, whose material is taught from A-level upwards – says unambiguously:

*If 'active' and 'passive' management styles are defined in sensible ways, it **must** be the case that:*

(1) Before costs, the return on the average actively managed dollar will equal the return on the average passively managed dollar and

(2) After costs, the return on the average actively managed dollar will be less than the return on the average passively managed dollar.

*These assertions will hold for **any** time period. Moreover, they depend only on the laws of addition, subtraction, multiplication and division. Nothing else is required.*

And then, to avoid doubt, he adds:

To repeat: Properly measured, the average actively managed dollar must underperform the average passively managed dollar, net of costs. Empirical analyses that appear to refute this principle are guilty of improper measurement.[9]

The principle really is that simple.

There are other advantages to passive investment:

- *No 'style drift'* – sometimes active managers will change their style – this may (or may not) knock into a cocked hat the reason for choosing the manager in the first place. Passive investors either have no style (!) or define their style academically and stick to it.

- *It is more understandable* – for those who own a passive portfolio, portfolio performance starts to make sense. This is very reassuring.

The most straightforward of passive approaches is to use pure index funds. This will typically produce results that are better than most competing solutions, but there are more refined solutions that avoid the disadvantages of indexing. We term these strategies '**smart indexing**'. (There is further information on this approach in Chapter 7.) Essentially, smart indexing adds patience and intelligence to index fund management.

3.6 What the really smart people think

Like much of this book, this chapter may call into question some deeply held beliefs. This is usually an uncomfortable process.

To help reassure you, here are a few choice quotations from the experts – a series of simple quotations from the world's most famous investors and professors that support our assertion.

Warren Buffett, widely regarded as one of the most successful investors and one of the world's wealthiest people, recommends that most investors should adopt the *7 Secrets* mantra of passive management. In the Chairman's Letter, 1996 Berkshire Hathaway Corp. Annual Report,[10] he said:

> *Most investors, both institutional and individual, will find that the best way to own common stocks is through an index fund that charges minimal fees.*

The late Merton Miller,[11] co-recipient of the 1990 Nobel Prize in Economic Sciences, wrote:

> *[Any] pension fund manager who doesn't have the vast majority – and I mean 70% or 80% of his or her portfolio – in passive investments is guilty of malfeasance, non-feasance or some other kind of bad feasance! There's just no sense for most of them to have anything but a passive investment strategy … Most pension fund managers cannot even reasonably hope to do any better than a passive fund. And on a risk adjusted basis they don't!*

The benefits of a passive approach over an active approach are widely acknowledged in the fund management industry and in the academic world. Private clients who wish to manage money prudently owe it to themselves or the ultimate beneficiaries of an investment to invest at least the bulk of their assets with these simple mathematical truisms in mind.

We hope that this weight of evidence from the smartest investors will convince you to question received wisdom and not even try to beat the market.

3.7 Conclusion

We have argued strongly in this chapter that you cannot beat the market in the long term, net of costs. Active management – the number-one investment strategy that the finance establishment has long urged us to follow – is not the best approach for the vast majority of small investors.

We understand that this information is difficult to absorb when first heard: it goes against everything we thought we knew about investment, or at least what the investment business would like us to believe. The sooner the truth is fully accepted by investors and advisers, the sooner we can take sensible decisions that will actually enable us to achieve our dreams.

We advocate giving up that hunt to find that elusive, brilliant investment manager. If you continue to engage in this futile search the result can only be frustration and disillusionment with investing.

Knowing that you and your advisers cannot predict or beat the market can be a relief. All we have to do is to devise a way of investing that acknowledges that we cannot predict the market.

A well-thought-out, passive approach to investment will tip the odds of success in your favour: as we explain in Chapter 7, you need to keep things simple and focus on the aspects you can control.

Risk is a primary driver, and it is risk that we focus on in the next chapter.

Secret no.

Some *financial risks* are really *not worth taking*

4.1 Introduction

This chapter lifts the veil on the important subject of risk, to help you make informed investment decisions for a more satisfactory return. By the end of the chapter you will have a sound understanding of the subject – you will probably be more educated about investment risk than many advisers. Give yourself that advantage when it comes to your own investments and you will learn how to avoid unnecessary risks.

A failure to understand risk can result in a lower return than an investor expected. In the most extreme cases you put yourself in danger of losing not just a substantial part but all of your investment – remember the Bernie Madoff, Enron and WorldCom examples.

When you are investing it is vitally important to consider the many different kinds of risk you could be exposing yourself to. Some risks are worth taking and some should be avoided at all costs. By the end of this chapter you will know the difference.

NB: This and the next chapter may at times seem rather technical, but we would encourage you to persevere. We want to keep things as straightforward as possible, but we feel that the information is so important and vital to your investing success that these chapters include some relatively complex material. Complete comprehension is not necessary, but an awareness of the issues will put you in a position to make more informed choices.

4.2 On risk and return

The concept of getting a return for taking risk is not new. In the Bible (Matthew 25: 14–30) two servants who take intelligent risks with money their master has given them are rewarded, while one who buries it in the ground because he is afraid of losing it is fiercely punished.

One of the basic ideas of investing is that there is no return without risk. That is why you would expect to get a higher return for owning shares than for, say, owning bonds in the issuing company.

A good example of this principle of receiving a greater return for taking a greater risk is from the television show *Dragons' Den*.[1] If the Dragons decide to invest in a company they consider 'risky', they will ask for a bigger share in the company than they would do in a company which they consider less risky. They expect to receive extra compensation for taking extra risk.

When building an investment portfolio you need to balance your requirement for return with the risk that you will need to take to earn that return. Generally speaking the higher the return you want or need the more risk you will need to take, but this is a double-edged sword. The fact that you are striving to earn a greater return will make the range of outcomes more uncertain.

Many investors and even advisers do not understand all of the risk involved in some of the financial products they are using. This lack of knowledge is dangerous and will leave you vulnerable to significant risk: you could be at risk of not having access to your money when you most need it or, even worse, the investment performing differently to your expectations. The complexity of many investment products today can be baffling, and as advisers we want to try to remove this complexity so that the risks you enter into are understandable.

If you come across anyone trying to sell a financial product which they try to tell you has lots of upside potential with minimal or no downside risk (structured products spring to mind – see Chapter 1), run a mile. Risks are present in any financial product, and the returns that are available to them are a compensation for some form of risk.

When it comes to investment, people tend to talk about risk in vague terms. Advisers will discuss how the value of certain types of investment is likely to fluctuate, while as an investor you are more likely to think of risk as the danger that you will lose money. Both are valid, but there are other elements of risk that you need to be aware of too.

Essentially risk is about dealing with the uncertainty that events in the future bring. The more you understand about the possible areas of uncertainty in investing, the easier it will be for you to deal with this uncertainty.

In the same way that going for a test drive does not tell you the full story about the issues you need to consider when you are buying a new car, a presentation from a financial adviser or fund salesman on costs and performance will not tell you the full story about the risks of investing.

In this chapter we will not try to help you analyse your own willingness or need to take risk (your financial adviser will guide you here). *We first want you to understand the types of risks you may be confronted with when building an investment portfolio.* In doing so we hope to show you that there are some risks that are worth taking and some that are really not – akin to running across a motorway: inherently dangerous with little chance of reward on the other side.

Some risks can be reduced, whereas there are others which may not at first appear evident, but which can have nasty consequences if they are not taken into account. By the end of the chapter you will know which risk is which and how to distinguish between them.

4.3 An explanation of different types of risk

When building an investment portfolio you will come up against
two main categories of risk:

- *Market risks:* These are risks generally associated with the
  nature and behaviour of the investment itself: for example,
  shares have different risks from bonds, and their price varies
  often, owing to factors affecting the whole stock market, not
  just the company itself.

- *Implementation risks:* This category covers the structure of
  how you invest: for example, the risks involved in using one
  type of fund as against another.

If you want control over your finances, it is important that you
understand the differences between the two and what can be done
about them. The diagram below shows these two types of risks
and their components:

Figure 3 *The two main types of investment risk and their components*

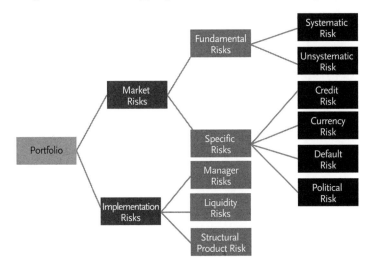

We will now look at each of these risks in turn.

4.4 Market risks

Market risks can also be split into two main types for the purposes of investing: *fundamental risks*, both systematic and unsystematic, and *more specific risks*, such as credit risk, currency risk and what we call default risk. We define these for you as follows:

Fundamental risks

Systematic risk

This is the risk that cannot be diversified away and is present in all markets. It is a general risk involved with all types of investment: the risk that investments can go up as well as down. There is nothing one can do to remove this risk, but it is one of the most important factors in terms of supplying returns.

- This is a risk which one gets rewarded for taking. It is the risk of putting your capital to work. As long as capitalism continues to function, systematic risk will provide investors with a return.

Unsystematic risk

This is the risk that a specific security or group of securities will be affected by an issue – for example, the impact on a company's share price of a strike by its employees. This risk can be diversified away by owning a large number of securities. This is one of the main reasons why we recommend investing in very broadly diversified funds.

It can seem attractive to invest heavily in an area where you believe you have some insight, such as the shares of the company you work for. While this may give you some perceived 'edge', you may not be in possession of all of the information that may influence the behaviour of that investment. Good examples of this are the employees of Enron and WorldCom, who lost billions of dollars in savings when their employers went bust, having invested heavily in their companies' shares.

■ Taking unsystematic risk does not get rewarded by extra return, but the risk can be reduced to insignificant levels by, for instance, spreading your stock market investments across many different companies – the funds we recommend as advisers often own many thousands of companies.

More specific risks

Credit risk

Credit risk is the risk that a company or individual will be unable to pay the contractual interest or principal on its debt obligations. This risk is a particular concern for people who hold bonds in their portfolio. Government bonds often but not always have much lower risk than those issued by companies, and thus pay lower interest. Bonds with a lower risk of defaulting are often referred to as 'investment grade'.

■ The best way of reducing credit risk is by diversifying your portfolio across a wide number of bonds. The type of bonds you invest in will depend upon your objectives and the role bonds are expected to play in your portfolio. We talk about this more in the next chapter, and it is a risk that can be worth taking if managed properly.

Currency risk

Movements in currency exchange rates can significantly affect the price of an asset in your home currency. This risk applies to all types of investment that are in a currency other than your home country currency. As an example, if you are a UK investor and invest in the US stock market, even though the share prices are rising you may see the value of your investment fall if the US dollar falls in value against the pound.

- The best way of reducing this risk is to have a wide range of currencies in those investments which can move up and down in price significantly, such as shares, while for those investments such as bonds which tend to fluctuate a lot less in price it is usually best to hedge any currency risk back to your home currency. This risk needs to be carefully managed. Taking currency risk in bonds is not generally a good idea if those bonds are to provide security to a portfolio. Currency movements can wipe out relatively modest bond returns overnight. In equities, currency risk is a different matter. In the USA, for instance, most of the earnings of the companies quoted in the S&P 500 are not in US dollars, and the impact of this will be reflected in the share price. If you are invested in a huge number of broadly diversified companies globally this risk balances out well over time.

Default risk

This refers to the risk that a country (or other institution) will be unable to honour its financial commitments – for example, paying interest or returning principal on bonds it has issued. The price of all financial instruments from that country will be affected. (The risk of a country defaulting as opposed to a company defaulting is sometimes known as sovereign risk.)

- This type of risk is most often seen in emerging markets (though we have seen recently that the developed Western world can also be vulnerable to default risk) and can best be reduced by diversifying your investments across a wide range of countries, thus minimising the impact this risk could potentially have.

Political risk

This represents the financial risk that a country's government will suddenly change its policies. This is a major reason for lack of foreign investment in developing countries.

- This is also a risk which can be diversified away by investing globally and not focusing on specific countries. It is also best if the funds that you use have some sort of policy as to how to handle this risk.

4.5 Implementation risks

Manager risks

When investing in funds you have to consider what risks are associated with using the fund manager. The fund manager's philosophy, process and results, and the way they are regulated, are among the factors that you need to consider. Thorough investigation of these and other factors can be a complex and time-consuming job and is not something to be undertaken lightly.

One of the best illustrations of this risk is how so many supposedly 'sophisticated' investors lost money in the Madoff fraud. It is vitally important that a manager meets certain minimum criteria for how they administer and account for client assets before it can be deemed safe to invest with them. It is important to ensure that either you or your adviser carries out a thorough investigation of the fund managers you are thinking of using and of how your money will be accounted for and managed. The rules and regulations governing unit trusts in Europe, for instance, are very strict, involving checks and balances at many different levels, whereas those governing structured products and some hedge funds, for example, are not as onerous. If you are in any doubt go for the more heavily regulated product.

- The best way to avoid these risks is by investing in low-cost passive funds that will provide you with the return of a particular benchmark or asset class that they are designed to emulate while being subject to extremely strict rules and regulations.

Liquidity risks

One of the biggest risks that an investor can face is not being able to access their investments when they are needed most. Life can bring many surprises, and access to one's investments at relatively short notice can from time to time be a necessity. If too many of your investments are in strategies which are relatively illiquid, you risk not being able to access money when you need it.

- You should always try to ensure that the bulk of your money is placed in investments that are extremely liquid and accessible as and when you need them.

The other side of liquidity risk is where you experience a sudden fall in the value of your investments just before you need to access them. This is more likely to happen if you have a high proportion of your investments in volatile assets such as equities.

- The best way to counter this risk is by ensuring that your spread of investments is appropriate to your needs. The vast majority of the investments that you are likely to need within the next two to three years should be in government bonds or other such low-risk assets, and most of the remainder of your portfolio should be held in funds that can be liquidated within a matter of a few days. There is little evidence to suggest there is extra return for tying your money up for long periods of time.

Structural product risk

Some investment products involve risks that may not be immediately clear to investors. These risks may also have been underestimated by the institutions responsible for the products. This is quite clearly demonstrated by the problems experienced by many institutions and investors recently thanks to products based upon sub-prime mortgages. This has also been the case for a large number of so-called structured products that have failed to deliver the results promised in their marketing (as discussed in Chapter 1, section 5).

- Before you invest make sure that you are comfortable with how the products you select function. Advisers have a duty to help you here. If you are not sure how you are likely to earn returns from an investment, do not make the investment.

As advisers, we are from time to time presented with products which, based on surface evidence, seem to offer extremely attractive risk-adjusted returns but have a relatively short track record.

- Until a product or investment strategy has been through a period of extreme stress it is difficult to establish all of the risks involved.

Another structural product risk is costs. Unfortunately many investment products are subject to high fees and charges, which minimise the chances of investors in those products earning a return greater than that which is likely on a high-interest rate bank account.

- Make sure that you understand all of the costs associated with the different types of investments you are considering making.

Your adviser should be able to describe all of the costs to you, and indeed is obliged to do so. The difference between paying 1% and 3% in charges on similar products can be dramatic.

The following graph shows that a difference of only 2% in annual fees can create almost a 100% difference between final portfolio values for an investment yielding 6.5% per annum over 30 years.

Figure 4 *The impact of costs and returns* [2]

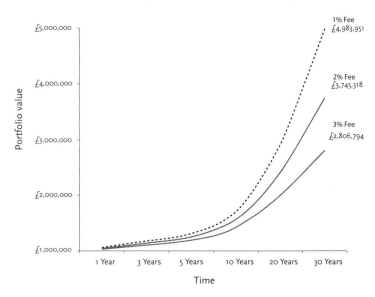

Assumed 6.5% Annualised Return over 30 Years

As we mentioned in the previous chapter, passive investments generally maintain lower fees than the average actively managed investment, by minimising trading costs and eliminating the costs of researching stocks.

- Where possible you should emphasise low-cost investments in your portfolio – there are enough high-quality funds available to make it unnecessary for you to take this risk.

4.6 Inflation

Inflation is a consistent risk to the real value of your investments. For the last decade or so we have become used to historically low levels of inflation; indeed governments have feared deflation. You need to make sure that you plan your investment strategy with a view to preserving the real value (i.e. the after inflation value) of your assets.

You will see in Secret 5 how we believe an intelligent combination of stocks and bonds will cope admirably with this risk. To show you exactly how damaging inflation can be to your wealth, consider the fact that you would need £3 today to buy what you could have bought with £1 in 1980.

Just keeping your money in the bank will see it eaten away by the effects of inflation. Only sensible long-term diversification will effectively protect you against this risk.

4.7 Human capital

One final risk worth bearing in mind when it comes to investing is the risk associated with your 'human capital'. This is defined as the present value of your future earnings so that the younger you are as an investor the higher your potential future earnings, and the higher your human capital.

Your total capital is the value of your human capital plus the value of your financial capital, i.e. your investments and savings. The younger you are, the higher the 'wealth' stored in your human capital and thus the higher the risk you can afford to take with your financial capital. We suggest that the younger you are, the higher the proportion of your assets you can afford to invest in 'riskier' equities. The proportion should be analysed, however, based upon personal risk preferences as well.

As you move towards retirement, your ability to recover from major losses to your financial capital diminishes, as you have less human capital with which to replace the losses. (This risk becomes of vital importance in relation to the approach we set out in Secret no. 6.)

4.8 Summary – putting risk and return together

From the sections above you will realise that there is a variety of risks involved with investment. We have tried to show that there are some risks worth taking, some which can be diversified away and others which are best avoided at all costs.

We suggest that you always analyse investments from the point of view of the risks we have discussed in this chapter. Careful analysis based on your new knowledge of risk is important to check whether the investments have merit.

Investments should be transparent and the risks involved easy to understand: if you feel you do not understand the risks fully, ask more questions until you are satisfied. As we will discuss in Chapter 7, investing can be a simple process: in general, avoid complicated investments. Not all of the risks are usually apparent, and it is usually the hidden risks which will hit you hardest and be least welcome.

Make sure you are properly rewarded for taking the risk of investing in equities over time through owning enough of them across as many markets as possible. For more on diversification, see the next chapter. As you will learn, bonds also provide a good return for the risk taken, provided you stick to the very highest quality bonds and keep their average lifetime relatively low.

SECRET NO.

Asset allocation is the most
crucial decision of all

5.1 Introduction

Source: Dilbert[1]

The major decision that you should concern yourself with is how to divide your investments between different types of assets.

Various academic studies[2] have shown that over 90% of the variability of returns is explained by strategic asset allocation – put simply, the proportion of shares (equities) and fixed interest (bonds) held. Active strategies – market timing and share selection – undertaken in an attempt to beat the market are repeatedly shown to have only a slight significance.

The usual cry from the media and the financial establishment goes along the lines of 'this year is the year to be in emerging market shares' … or commodities or property or some other kind of investment. They try to encourage investors to move money into whichever arena they feel they can best promote with a slick marketing story.

You are probably well aware by now that we have no truck with this attempt at crystal ball gazing – it encourages far too much activity on the part of the investor and costs far too much in fees.

We believe that by following a sensibly devised plan whereby you spread your assets across a number of appropriate investments and keep the proportions allocated to those various investments in balance, you will give yourself the best possible chance of meeting your investment goals.

This chapter shows you how to achieve this aim.

5.2 Spreading your investments

Of all the decisions you make as an investor, the one which is likely to have the greatest influence on your investing success, or lack of it, is how you divide your wealth between the different types of investments available to you.

This process of spreading your investments, referred to by the industry as asset allocation, is nothing new. In a famous textbook devoted purely to the subject, Roger Gibson, an expert in the field,[3] illustrated the concept with a quotation from the Talmud:

> *Let every man divide his money into three parts, and invest a third in land, a third in business, and a third let him keep in reserve.*

The suggestion that one should spread one's investments is seen by many to be good common sense in terms of reducing risk, but it can also be a valuable tool to help you increase the return on your investments if you follow a disciplined process.

5.3 Narrowing down your asset options

Investment at its simplest level is principally concerned with either owning an asset or equity stake, or lending your capital.

There are two fundamental ways of getting a return on capital:

- Owning commercial enterprises or assets such as equities or property, with the potential of receiving dividends, rent or some other ownership reward.

- Lending your capital to a government or company by purchasing a gilt or bond (fixed-interest investment) and receiving interest.

The returns derived from these two general types of assets are sufficient for your portfolio; there is no imperative for you to look elsewhere. Any investment in which one of these two sources of return is not apparent should be viewed with scepticism as it will normally fall into the speculation category, involving some form of forecasting of the future of asset prices.

There are two main areas where you should focus your investments:

a) Bonds

As we mentioned in the previous chapter, bonds come in a number of different varieties and with different levels of risk attached to them. The level of risk is based on the creditworthiness of the institution issuing the bonds and its ability to pay the coupon (interest) due on those bonds. One other factor which comes into play is the maturity of the bonds – in other words, when they are due to pay back their capital value.

Figure 5 *Risks and returns in bond investing*[A]

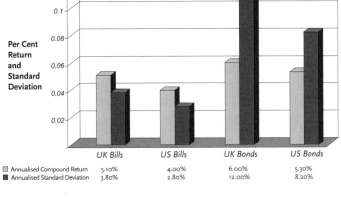

Fixed Interest, Extending Maturities

	UK Bills	US Bills	UK Bonds	US Bonds
☐ Annualised Compound Return	5.10%	4.00%	6.00%	5.30%
■ Annualised Standard Deviation	3.80%	2.80%	12.00%	8.20%

Figure 5 looks at 100 years of data. It compares the return on US and UK bills with the returns on UK and US bonds. In this context both bills and bonds are loans to the government:

- Bills are usually short-term loans of twelve months or less.

- Bonds are longer-term loans that can range from 3 to 50 years. In the UK, government bonds are also known as gilts.

As an investor, you might expect that if you lent a government or business money for long periods you would get a better return than if you lent the same organisation money in the short term.

The evidence does not support this contention. If you bought 'bonds' then the return (the light bars on the graph) hardly rises at all compared to bills; the volatility (the dark bars), however, goes up hugely. So you get roughly the same return in the end but in a rather scarier fashion. The data demonstrates the same outcome for loans to non-government bodies such as businesses.

The sensible conclusion, then, is probably not to lend your money to governments or companies for long periods of time because on average you are not well rewarded. You might as well lend them your money over shorter periods and garner roughly the same return with less pain.

So, *when investing in bonds, look to invest in short-term bonds to get the best risk–return ratio.* As ever, you should seek to diversify: own a large number of bonds rather than one particular bond.

Investors generally hold bonds for one of two reasons:

1. To reduce overall portfolio volatility (the swings in value of a portfolio).

2. To generate a reliable income stream.

These objectives typically lead to different investment decisions. The first approach, volatility reduction, is an application of what is known as the 'separation theorem' (i.e., hold equities for higher return and use fixed income to temper portfolio volatility). Rather than increasing risk to maximise yield, investors adopting this approach want to hold bonds that have a lower risk. Certain types of bonds, particularly shorter-term government bonds, are better suited for this strategy.

With this in mind, some long-term investors may seek to earn higher expected returns by shifting risk to the equity side of their portfolio. With an eye to minimising maturity and credit risk, they hold short-term, high-quality debt instruments that have historically offered lower yields with much lower volatility.

The second purpose of holding bonds is to generate reliable cash flow. Income-oriented investors, such as pensioners, may not worry as much about short-term volatility in their bond portfolio. If you are in this situation your priority is to meet a specific income (or cash-flow) need in the future. Consequently, you might wish to design a portfolio around bonds and accept more volatility in hope of earning higher yields, through holding bonds with longer maturities and/or lower credit quality. Be careful here: this is a complex area.

Whether investing for total long-term return or for income, a portfolio should be diversified across bonds and global markets to avoid the risk of having too much money invested in one bond issuer and to take advantage of differing global interest rates. More often than not investors should seek to invest in bonds denominated in their home currency or in funds that invest globally, but remove this currency risk through a process of currency hedging.

b) Equities

You are likely to gain a considerable extra return from taking the extra risk involved in equities. To explain this, it is useful to extend the concepts of systematic and unsystematic risk discussed in Secret 4:

- **Unsystematic risks** are risks specific to a company or industry. These risks might involve such things as a lawsuit or a fraud, or, in the case of an industry, changes in legislation or strikes. You can diversify these risks away by owning shares in lots of different companies and across many different industries. These risks are not worth taking and you receive no compensation for them as an investor.

- **Systematic risk** is the risk that comes with being invested in the stock market. You cannot diversify away this risk, which encompasses such things as war, recession and inflation. It is however a risk you receive a reward for. It is a risk worth taking.

Figure 6 *Risks of equity investing*[5]

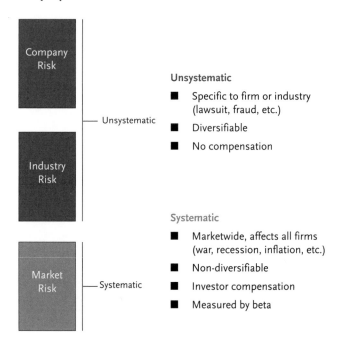

Total Equity Risk

Company Risk	
Industry Risk	— Unsystematic
Market Risk	— Systematic

Unsystematic

■ Specific to firm or industry (lawsuit, fraud, etc.)

■ Diversifiable

■ No compensation

Systematic

■ Marketwide, affects all firms (war, recession, inflation, etc.)

■ Non-diversifiable

■ Investor compensation

■ Measured by beta

As you will appreciate from our descriptions of the different types of risk, you will quite quickly destroy your advantage if you take risks that are not rewarded – for example, by investing in too few companies or trying to pick a specific industry that you think will do well (think back to the internet mania of the late 1990s if you ever get tempted to do this!).

You get rewarded for investing in the stock market as a whole. As demonstrated by the Nobel Prize-winning work of Professor Bill Sharpe of Stanford,[6] this strategy is responsible for roughly 70% of the returns you get for investing in equities over time.

In 1992 academics Eugene Fama and Ken French[7] looked at whether there were other ways of explaining the returns that one gets from equity investing. The results of their work are extremely interesting. They found that by analysing firstly the size of a company related to the other companies in the market, and secondly the price of a company related to the book value of its assets, you could explain 96% of the variability of returns in equities.

This may sound somewhat technical, but for the investor it has two very important implications. Fama and French's research showed that:

- Investors have received a higher return for investing in small companies (small cap) compared to big companies.

- You get a higher return for investing in companies whose prices are low compared to the book value of their assets (value companies) than investing in growth companies.

Investing in smaller-value companies is a risk that one seems to get rewarded for over time, and the extra reward can be quite significant.

Over time and across many different markets around the world a pattern emerges. Large-value companies give investors a higher return than large companies in general, and significantly higher than large-growth companies. This pattern repeats across different sizes of company, with small-value companies having higher returns than small-growth companies, and small-value companies having even higher returns than their large-value counterparts. (See Appendix 4 for a chart showing size and value effects on equity returns in markets around the world.)

Think of it this way: value beats growth and small beats large.

How can you distinguish a 'value' company from a 'growth' company?

As we stated above, one of the ways to measure value and growth is by looking at the value of a company's assets compared with its market price. Often the growth companies are seen as being industry or market leaders. They are the types of companies which receive a lot of positive focus in the press and also from stock market analysts. Value companies are often seen as being out of favour. The general market view is often negative on these companies, and bad news is factored into their price. The share prices of growth companies tend to rise substantially in value whereas value companies experience a declining price.

A good example is a previous darling of the UK stock market, BP. When the Deepwater Horizon disaster occurred in 2010, BP's share price fell dramatically and the overwhelming focus was on bad news. BP still had enormous assets, however, and as the share price fell, BP became what could be seen as a 'value' company. If you invested in BP when all the news was negative, you were buying assets much more cheaply than had previously been possible, and your opportunity for a good return was much higher.

You should, however, bear in mind that the higher expected returns of small and value companies do not happen every year: you may have to remain invested for a number of years to fully realise the benefits of investing in these types of equities.

A better approach would perhaps be to invest in very broadly diversified whole-of-market funds that have additional exposure to these risk factors.

5.4 Your investment split

So, how should you divide your investments between equities and bonds? What proportions will ensure the best returns?

A common method is to evaluate a number of different portfolios (most good advisers will have various 'model' portfolios with differing allocations to different investments) in terms of their risk and return characteristics:

■ A riskier portfolio holds 100% equities.

■ The least volatile portfolio holds 100% bonds.

■ Between these extremes lie standard equity–bond allocations, such as 80%–20%, 60%–40%, 40%–60% and 20%–80%.

Then you compare the average annualised return and volatility (standard deviation) of each model portfolio for different periods, such as one, three, five, ten and twenty years.

Volatility is one of several risk measures investors may want to consider, showing how much portfolio value is likely to fluctuate over time. With this in mind, the analysis should feature average returns, as well as best- and worst-case returns, for the various periods.

The following table gives examples of a range of portfolios from a portfolio with 100% equities (column 1) to a portfolio with 100% bonds (column 6)

Figure 7 *Portfolio application ranges*[8]

Model Portfolios

	Equity	Aggressive	Normal	Moderate	Conservative	Fixed
FTSE All-Share Index	20%	16%	12%	8%	4%	-
MSCI UK Value Index (gross div.)	15%	12%	9%	6%	3%	-
MSCI UK Small Cap Index (gross div.)	15%	12%	9%	6%	3%	-
MSCI World ex UK Index (gross div.)	15%	12%	9%	6%	3%	-
MSCI World ex UK Value Index (gross div.)	15%	12%	9%	6%	3%	-
MSCI Emerging Markets Index (gross div.)	10%	8%	6%	4%	2%	-
MSCI World Small Cap Index (gross div.)	10%	8%	6%	4%	2%	-
UK One-Month Treasury Bills	-	20%	40%	60%	80%	100%
Total	**100%**	**100%**	**100%**	**100%**	**100%**	**100%**

FTSE data courtsey of FTSE. MSCI data copyright MSCI 2010, all rights reserved

While this technique relies on historical performance that may not be repeated in the future, and does not consider various investment costs, it may help you think about the risk–return trade-off and visualise the range of potential outcomes based on the aggressiveness of your strategy.

A good adviser will help you find the right balance and the right portfolio to reflect your approach to risk and return.

5.5 Refining your equity allocation

After establishing the basic equity–bond mix, investors should turn their attention to the equity allocation, which is where the best opportunities to refine the risk–return trade-off are found. Investors who are comfortable with a higher level of equity risk can overweight or 'tilt' their allocation towards riskier asset classes that have a history of offering average returns above the market.

We have talked about the research published by Eugene Fama and Ken French.[9] This found that shares of smaller companies (small cap) have had higher average returns than those of large companies (large cap), and that so-called shares in 'value' companies provide investors with higher average returns than shares in 'growth' companies.

To recap: we define value companies as those companies whose share price is low compared to the value of the company's assets. Conversely, growth companies are those whose share price is high compared to their assets.

By holding a larger portion of small-cap and value equities than mainstream indices or a typical portfolio, an investor increases the potential to earn higher returns for the additional risk taken.

The following graph shows the outperformance of small-cap and value shares compared with the FTSE All Share Index, which measures the performance of main market shares in the UK.

Figure 8 *Returns on different asset classes in the UK, 1956–2013*[10]

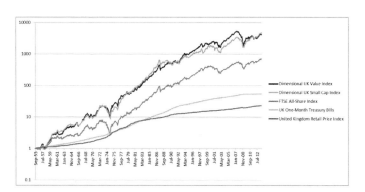

The final step in refining the equity component is to diversify globally. By holding an array of equity asset classes across domestic and international markets, investors can reduce the impact of underperformance in a single market or region of the world. While the relationship of returns in various markets may vary over time, this diversification can further reduce volatility in a portfolio, which translates into higher compounded returns over time.

While it can seem comforting to invest a large portion of your equity exposure in your home market, this may not always be the best idea from a risk diversification point of view. Those investors who live in a country that has a large stock market have better opportunities to diversify than those who live in countries with relatively small stock markets. Regardless of where you live, however, diversification is always worthwhile.

5.6 Taking the process further with diversification

We make reference to diversification in the section above.

This is the powerful 'not putting all your eggs in one basket' approach to investment.

One of the issues often mentioned recently is that investment in the main US stock market index, the S&P 500, has been essentially flat over the last ten years. While this may be true in the US, it certainly is not true of all markets.

Indeed, by spreading your investments globally across a number of different types of markets you would have fared a lot better than by betting on just one market. This process of spreading your investments across different types of investments (equities and bonds, for example) and/or across markets is what we commonly refer to as diversification. Diversification will help you improve returns and help protect you against the worst ravages of market falls.

The process of diversification involves two basic elements which were detailed by academic and Nobel laureate James Tobin[11] in the late 1950s. His 'separation theorem' proposes that all investors face two important decisions:

1. Deciding how much risk to take, and then;

2. Building a portfolio of 'risky' assets (equities) and 'less risky' assets (bonds) to achieve this risk exposure.

So by adding bonds to a portfolio of equities you can reduce the risk of a portfolio. The greater the bond allocation relative to equities, the less risky the portfolio and the lower the total expected return; the greater the equity allocation relative to bonds, the higher the portfolio's expected return and risk.

This, of course, presumes that you own the right type of bonds in your portfolio. Here we are mainly referring to bonds of very high quality, or 'investment grade' as they are often called.

5.7 How has diversification worked in practice?

The last few years have shown the benefits of sensible asset allocation to many investors. A large number also discovered that in chasing higher returns they were living with more risk and potential for large losses when markets headed south in 2008. Bill Sharpe was once asked which sort of investment was likely to have the highest return. His response was that it was likely to be the investment that would give you the worst returns in 'down' markets.

If you were to analyse portfolio mixes similar to those we showed earlier in this chapter (Figure 7, page 85), over the period 1999–2013 you would see the following:

■ The annualised returns would show that the portfolio with the highest level of risk through exposure to the stock market had the highest level of return (7.42% per annum). It was almost the most volatile of all the portfolios (standard deviation of 15.82%).

■ The portfolio with the highest level of bonds not only had the lowest level of risk as measured by volatility (1.07%) but also the lowest level of return (3.42% per annum).

Looking at the full range of returns from a certain type of portfolio will help you more than purely looking at its average performance. Using the portfolios described above you would probably have been most attracted by the higher average return of the portfolio with the largest percentage of equities, but how comfortable would you have felt with that portfolio's return of −32.67% in 2008?[12]

Think of it as crossing a river: you need to know the depth of the river all the way across, not just its average depth. The average depth may be four feet, but if for most of the way across it is only a foot deep but suddenly drops to eight feet halfway, you may find yourself in difficulty, particularly if you cannot swim.

Beware of averages – they do not tell you about the full range of risks, and you should explore how you can cope with the full range of returns a portfolio is likely to offer.

For a more complete illustration of the types of returns you can expect on the portfolios described in this chapter, please see Appendix 1. This will give you an idea of what it would feel like to hold our recommended index-based portfolios.

5.8 Introducing other types of risk and return

So far we have talked mainly about splitting a portfolio between shares and bonds, but what about other types of investments?

Between the four advisers writing this book, we have at one stage or another probably come across just about every type of investment you could imagine, including, for example, property, commodities, high-yield bonds, hedge funds, private equity funds … the list goes on and on.

We have all, however, over the last few years, reached the conclusion (some after more research than others!) that *bonds and equities should be the main components of every portfolio*. There may be room for a couple of other types of investment, such as property and maybe even commodities, but apart from these two types of investment nothing else will give you the same portfolio benefits, at a low cost, and in a reliable manner, as shares and bonds.

There are essentially four key asset classes. These are businesses, property, cash and debt. Businesses and property have produced far better long-term returns than the other two asset classes. In this book we have devoted little time to property. The main reason is that many of our clients are already very well exposed to property as homeowners, buy-to-let investors and commercial property owners.

For those with relatively little of their wealth tied up in property, there are low-cost index funds available that can give access to some types of property investing. This is something to be discussed with your adviser in light of your existing property ownership.

The risks of most other types of investment do not, in our opinion, and in the opinion of overwhelming academic research, make sense. While on paper they may seem to present attractive returns with claims of relatively low levels of risk, these rewards do not present themselves in reality. The costs of most other forms of investment are dramatically higher than those of investing in shares and bonds and present the investor with a high hurdle to jump before they have earned any return. As you will see in the chapter on risk and return, in order to get a higher return, you have to take a higher level of risk, regardless of what some smooth-talking salesman or fancy advert might tell you.

The best way to decide which types of investment are right for you is to discuss it with an adviser, but our advice would be that if he starts talking about anything other than passively managed investments in anything other than bonds, shares and perhaps property and commodities, take your money elsewhere.

5.9 A word on rebalancing

While spreading your investments between bonds and equities can help you adjust the risk of your portfolio and thus its likely returns, it is important that you maintain this risk level over time, or your portfolio may move out of balance and become subject to a higher level of risk than you wished. You can keep balance in your portfolio by using a process known as rebalancing. The basic idea is that once an asset class has moved up in value you should sell some of your investments in this asset class and buy investments in the asset class which has in comparison done less well, to a level that maintains your originally agreed risk levels. It is important not to rebalance too often and not to incur significant costs.

5.10 Getting the most from your portfolio

The equity–bond decision drives a large part of your portfolio's long-term performance. During portfolio design, evaluating different equity–bond combinations can help you visualise the risk–return trade-off as you consider the range of potential outcomes over time. Once you determine a mix, it can guide more detailed choices of asset classes to hold in the portfolio. And as your appetite for risk shifts over time, you can revisit the mix to estimate how shifting your portfolio mix may affect your wealth accumulation goals in the future.

As a rule of thumb, the younger you are the more you can afford to invest in the equity markets, given that you have many years of earning potential ahead of you and therefore, should your portfolio suffer a significant fall in value, you have the opportunity to replace these losses with increased saving over time, which is an opportunity that may not be available to someone nearing the end of their career. An overall rule of thumb that many investors have used successfully is to allocate the same percentage as their age to bonds in their portfolio. Thus as they get older they increase the proportion of their assets allocated to the more stable element of the portfolio – high-quality bonds. This is, however, a rule of thumb, and as such needs to be treated with caution.

Other factors should be taken into account when determining how you diversify your assets. The overall size of your investment portfolio will, for instance, play a role in influencing your capacity for and desire to take risk. For many, a requirement for the portfolio to generate an income or flow of cash payments could also be crucial, particularly as you reach retirement age and may depend upon your investment portfolio to help maintain your standard of living.

Taking all of the above factors into account, as well as your own natural propensity for taking or avoiding risk, an analysis of likely portfolio behaviour should help you find a split of investments with which you feel comfortable. The final factor in helping to ensure that you get the best out of your portfolio is **discipline**.

Managing a portfolio is somewhat like piloting a plane. At the outset you decide upon your destination and how quickly and at what altitude you are going to fly to get there. Along the way, however, you will need to make small adjustments to your course because of winds, storms and the like which may cause you to deviate. By staying disciplined and following the agreed course as closely as possible you give yourself the greatest possible opportunity of arriving comfortably on time at your destination.

5.11 Conclusion

We hope that this chapter on asset allocation gives you a useful framework for constructing a portfolio that will meet your needs. Sadly, even with this we know that investors still face a significant challenge. Despite our best intentions we often let our emotions get in the way of sensible investment decisions. The next chapter discusses how our behaviour affects our investing success. Read on if you want to avoid the most common pitfalls to which we are all prone.

SECRET NO.

Your behaviour
will define
your return

6.1 Introduction

95% of wealth creation comes from your behaviour, and 5% from your investments.[1]

Most investment theory and advice is based on the premise that our behaviour around money is based on rational thought and action. We all like to think of ourselves as rational beings, for after all, is that not what separates us from the rest of the animal kingdom?

Not so when it comes to investing. We humans are pre-programmed to respond emotionally and not rationally: we are just not wired for prudent, long-term investing. Issues around finance appeal to our base emotions – often the wrong emotions: fear and greed. This leads us to damaging behaviour such as taking too much risk in the hope that we hit that elusive jackpot.

The very greatest risk to a portfolio is client behaviour, since in a moment of anxiety the client can entirely wipe out their carefully chosen asset allocation.

This chapter takes information from the fascinating and comparatively new area of behavioural finance. Using this approach, we describe the most common forms of behavioural bias we all face and show how these can influence our investment decision-making.

This chapter describes our most costly investment behaviours.

With knowledge and discipline we can all learn to control our instincts for a better investment outcome. No plan is going to survive the vicissitudes of life without a real understanding of how you relate to money. When things start to go wrong, and go wrong they will, it is important that you understand how you are hard-wired to act and take that understanding into account before you act. You run the risk of your plans being sabotaged by your subconscious beliefs. Acquiring this knowledge and discipline is very difficult to do unaided.

This chapter ends with an impassioned plea to seek the assistance of an experienced financial guide to help you control your natural inclinations and achieve your goals.

6.2 Our natural biases can be our worst enemy

Investor behaviour has a massive impact on investment returns: your discipline, propensity to save and thought processes when faced with tough choices – all these inclinations will affect how you approach financial decisions.

Figure 9 *Average US stock fund return vs. average US stock fund investor, 1988–2007* [2]

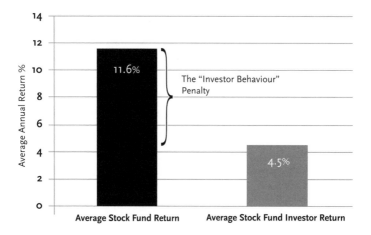

The recognition that investors can exhibit biased decision-making dates back at least as far as the early 1700s:

> *I can calculate the motion of heavenly bodies, but not the madness of people.*
>
> Sir Isaac Newton[3]

Here, Newton was referring to one of the earliest instances of a speculative run on a stock, in this case the South Sea Company. His intelligence could not save him from the 'herd instinct', however, and he eventually succumbed, losing £20,000, equivalent to £1 million in today's terms. The rise and subsequent collapse of the stock was fuelled by fierce rumours, fraud and the widespread use of leverage.

It would seem that speculation, at least in hindsight, has not changed much in the last 300 years. But, just as today, if investors then had recognised that they were gripped by greed and not reason, they could have avoided getting caught up in this particular bubble.

Individuals are 'wired' to make decisions by using their own behavioural biases. As we discuss later, this wiring is necessary for us to go about our daily lives. With investments, however, these instincts can lead to poor decision-making and a bad investment experience.

The media and the financial services industry both routinely prey on these biases and emotions. So as investors, what we require is not a cure, but a systematic process to take behavioural biases into account and a plan to control them.

Most investment theory is based on the assumption that investors are completely rational. They make decisions with the objective of maximising their wealth and are constrained only by their tolerance for bearing risk.

Not true, according to behaviourists,[4] who believe that many stock market investors act far from rationally. We know from our many years of experience just how true this is.

When faced with risky decisions, often our 'emotion overwhelms reason'. To put this another way, our behavioural biases can trump rational thought.

Recent research has shown that 'Financial losses are processed in the same areas of the brain that respond to mortal danger'.[5]

6.3 Six examples of behavioural bias

We are all prone to certain types of biases and behaviours when it comes to matters of finance. Here are the six most common and costly behaviours that can impede your ability to realise your goals. Study these with care, as it is likely that you will have suffered from them all at one point or another.

Behavioural bias 1 – inertia and regret avoidance

Do you recognise any of these excuses?

- It is all too complicated.
- How do I know who to trust?
- I will be all right as I am.
- What if I invest and it all goes wrong?
- All I read about is when things go wrong; I do not know where to start.
- I have no time to plan for my future; I live for today.

We often avoid making decisions for fear they will result in failure.

This type of inertia and avoidance is a very common trait and probably the most damaging of all behaviours we see. It has the potential to stop a person investing at all, halting engagement in proper financial planning – which ironically is the only way *not* to regret financial decisions.

Behavioural bias 2 – slave to fashion (or 'herding')

- Do you get your investment tips from friends and family or at the golf club?

Humans are influenced by what everyone else is doing or buying – there is comfort in being part of a group. How else can we explain why flared trousers were in fashion in the 1970s and out by the 1980s? Nuclear shelters were the must-have in the 1960s but are almost unheard of now, at a time when the number of nuclear weapons and countries holding them, and the risk of a dirty bomb, have grown significantly.

The problem is that 'fashionable' stocks and bonds are not like trouser styles or any other fashion, as they cannot be manufactured fast enough to keep up with demand, so popular stock and bond prices rise to reflect limited supply.

Conventional investment wisdom is usually wrong – if everyone believes that particular stocks are the best investment, that tells you that everyone owns them. This in turn means two things:

- First, because everyone has bought them, demand and therefore prices are high and future expected returns are low.

- Secondly, there are very few buyers left to purchase these stocks, as it is only when there are plenty of future buyers that prices can rise.

If the herd moves in one direction, it might be time to consider moving the other way.

Behavioural bias 3 – overconfidence

Researchers in cognitive psychology have shown that we all tend to be overconfident about our beliefs and abilities and over-optimistic about assessments of the future.

Ask a large group of drivers about their competence in relation to the average driver in the group. In the case of college students, 80–90% of respondents invariably say that they are more skilful, safer drivers than the others. Clearly this cannot be the case.

In the same way, most investors believe that they can beat the market and they tend to speculate too much and trade too much, incurring ever-increasing costs. This is the foundation of the active management industry and leads investors to buy high and sell low, with the average investor experiencing the sort of below-market returns we detailed in Chapter 2.

It is not just investors; finance professionals are also prone to this behavioural bias, as Kristopffer Eriksen and Ola Kvaløy argue in their 2010 study, 'Myopic investment management':

> … *the important insight from our experiment is that the [financial] advisers' knowledge of the stock market and risk does not free them from myopic behaviour, but actually makes them more prone to it!*[6]

As we detail again in Chapter 7, your investment strategy should remove as much human interference as possible.

Behavioural bias 4 – hindsight bias

■ You just knew that a stock would double in a matter of days.

The illusion of financial skill may well stem from another physiological finding called 'hindsight bias', which refers to our tendency to see events that have already occurred as more predictable than they were before they took place. Hindsight promotes the illusion that the future is far more predictable than it is. We can all be wise after the event, but can we really trust our ability to consistently carry out the right action before we have the benefit of hindsight?

Another way that hindsight can become a problem is the assumption that the immediate past is predictive of the long-term future. This is called 'recency' or 'extrapolation'.[7] It is responsible for making investors buy stocks when prices are going up and stops them buying stocks or even selling them when prices have been going down.

In good times people are often willing to take risks in the belief that markets that have just increased will continue to do so. In bad times, uncertainties in the economy increase and people are afraid of taking risks. As a consequence:

■ Most people will try to invest in safe assets, and risk aversion increases. A 'flight to quality' takes place and investors tend to buy government gilts and the biggest, 'safest' companies.

■ Unless risk premiums (the likely additional reward for taking risk over taking little or no risk) are higher, nobody will invest in risky assets.

■ Therefore, to attract investors to risky assets, expected risk premiums should increase during bad economic times and the opposite is true in good economic times.

Business cycles and risk premiums

Figure 10 *Model illustrating how the cycle of risk premiums (expected future return) in equities is in opposition to the business cycle*

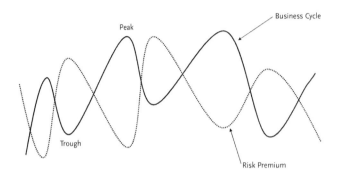

As Figure 10 shows, future expected returns on equities are lower when economic conditions are strong and higher when economic conditions are weak.[8] This contradicts most investors' preference to 'buy high and sell low'. A sensible rebalancing strategy provides the ongoing discipline necessary to sell high and buy low (see Chapter 5).

Behavioural bias 5 – the self-attribution bias

Our 'self-attribution bias' means that we tend to want to take full credit for success, but blame failures on outside influences.

Invariably, every market comes with its share of 'pundits' who called it correctly. Normally, we hear about how smart they were to look at evidence that others ignored. This is a natural by-product of being overconfident. Perhaps you were prescient enough to invest in Microsoft before it went public. On the other hand, perhaps you were an investor in Enron, believing the analysts, auditors and management of one of the most innovative companies of its time.

On average, we are all average – and make an average number of smart decisions and mistakes. Individually, however, we all think we were 'smart' when things work in our favour and 'unlucky' when things work against us.

The truth is that good or bad investment outcomes are based, in large part, on what news just came out: what we do not have knowledge of is what tomorrow's news will bring.

Behavioural bias 6 – where is the excitement?

If indexing or passive investment works so well, why do so few investors take advantage of it? Most likely because it is so dull!

One of the most deadly investment traps is the need for excitement. Humans routinely exchange large amounts of money for excitement. Gambling is thought to be the second-most enjoyable activity; why else do people flock to Las Vegas and Ascot or bet online when they know that on average they will end up with less than they started with? Why do people bet on anything but the favourite? Why do people buy a lottery ticket with impossibly low odds?

Do not confuse long-term investing with short-term speculating. Speculate with money you can afford to lose; invest with money for which it is essential to retain purchasing power.

In looking at various studies of investor behaviour, like the Lukas Schneider study mentioned previously, investors are either systematically bad gamblers, or they are succumbing to the behavioural biases that lead to poor investment decision-making. Or it is a combination of both.

Ultimately we are naturally attracted to the sweet and fatty foods, but what we need is a balanced meal which is not always so exciting, filling or immediately gratifying.

6.4 How can we control our natural biases?

You will understand from this chapter that we are all subject to certain behavioural biases when it comes to investing, but traits such as investing only in what is popular or seeing investment as a source of excitement are not conducive to a successful investment experience.

How do we learn to control these biases for a better investment outcome? There are three factors here:

1. The first part of the answer is to *recognise the biases we are prone to*: we hope this chapter has helped you do just that. Following on from this, we advise you to take a good hard look at your own personal attitudes and behaviours around money. Most approaches to managing your money jump in at the 'planning what you need to do' stage. We know from experience that unless you *do the exploration first*, your chances of achieving success subsequently are slim. First understand the drivers and how to react to them; then you will be in a position to make money work for you and do the job it was designed to do.

If you don't know who you really are, the stock market is an expensive place to find out

'Adam Smith' (George J. W. Goodman)[9]

Before you make a change to your finances, spend a bit of time understanding your particular relationship with money – your behaviour patterns, your feelings around money and where these attitudes come from. Then work out what you want money to achieve for you in your life.

2. The second part of the answer is to *implement the right type of investment strategy, recognising what you can control and what you can't.* If you implement the strategy we recommend in this book you will have far more control over your natural biases and traits. Chapter 7 sums this up for you.

3. The third part is to *keep the discipline of the investment strategy* and not to be fooled by the media or friends into thinking that you or anyone you are likely to meet can predict the future.

We will all continue to battle with our natural biases. Understanding your personal inclinations will allow you to begin to properly identify those things which you cannot control, but it is very difficult to accomplish this on your own, without a good 'steward' in your corner.

Finding the right financial guide to assist you in developing and sticking to a proper financial plan is a vital contributor to success.

6.5 You cannot do this by yourself – seek professional help

> *At the end of our investing lifetime, it won't matter what your funds did, it will matter what you did. And what you did will be a pure function of the quality of the advice you got – from one caring, competent adviser, and not from any number of magazines.*

> Nick Murray[10]

When it comes to your finances, recognising your natural inclinations and common behavioural traps is one thing; having the discipline to resist them is another. This is virtually impossible to do by yourself. We passionately believe that you need a skilled professional on your side through the process – someone who will keep you honest and focused during your financial journey, particularly when things get tough. It is just too hard to do it alone.

Finding the right financial guide or mentor is probably the single most important practical step you can take to start to use the information in this book effectively and implement a successful financial plan.

The right guide will coach you through the process and reinforce the discipline you will need to avoid the temptations that our natural behavioural biases and other forces conspire to lead us towards.

Proper financial planning with an expert guide provides the confidence and clarity you need to achieve financial peace of mind. We see clients who have put off this type of planning for years, but once the plan is in place, with appropriate professional assistance, it can take as little as two hours a year to review and maintain.

If you are serious about managing your wealth and achieving your long-term goals, seek the assistance of a professional.

6.6 The right type of financial guide – skilled, independent and easy to work with

Selecting the right guide to assist you is crucial. An important word here is *'independent'*. Many financial advisers are linked to a particular product provider or bank, rewarded on a commission basis by those providers. Even the private client banks set up to service wealthy people tend to sell their own products. While they term themselves 'independent financial advisers', in reality they are anything but.

There is a group of advisers who are truly independent. These are *independent fee-based advisers and financial planners*, legally required to put their clients' interests first. They see their role not as finding you 'market-beating' investments but in making you a better investor.

Another important word is *'skilled'*. Today markets are global and complex. Finance professionals will use their knowledge and specialist resources to help you build and maintain a carefully balanced portfolio, properly diversified with minimal fee and tax implications.

The guide you choose must be *someone with whom you can work*, who will advise you along the way. A good adviser needs not just to be competent technically in investments and planning but also to have good interpersonal skills and an excellent understanding of human behaviour and emotions around money. A good guide will help you define your true inner goals, identify your key behavioural strengths and struggles and 'financial personality'.[11]

Your chosen adviser should be an objective sounding board: someone you can talk all manner of financial and lifestyle choices through with. They should be able to give you the ongoing confidence and discipline to stick to your plan.

Sound financial advice is about understanding your personal objectives and circumstances and working together to help you formulate a future planning strategy to achieve these goals. Any discussion on particular products or investments is left to the end of the process, firmly anchored to those goals. A good guide will regularly review and tweak your plan as necessary to keep you on track.

(See Appendix 2 for a list of questions to help you select the right financial adviser.)

6.7 Be clear about your long-term goals

In any discussion about money and how best to make it work for you, you have to decide what you are trying to achieve with the money, and what it is you are trying to do.

A good financial guide will help you here.

The best way to start is to ask yourself a series of questions which will help you explore your life and the journey you are on.[12]

Three powerful questions to help you uncover your goals

Question 1: *Imagine that you are financially secure, that you have enough money to take care of your needs, now and in the future: how would you live your life? Would you change anything?*

Let yourself go. Do not hold back on your dreams. Describe a life that is complete, that is richly yours.

The beauty of this question is that it really asks you to envision what you would like to have, be and do in your life when there are no obstacles in terms of want and scarcity. The question enables you to put all this aside, all the things that hold you back from being, doing and having what you think you want. In fact we tend to be so inhibited that we do not really think about what it is that we want our lives to be about. So do not hold back; think big, and write down all these wonderful things that you want to do.

Question 2: *You visit your doctor, who tells you that you have only five to ten years left to live. The good part is that you will not ever feel sick. The bad news is that you will have no advance warning of the moment of your death. What will you do in the time you have remaining? Will you change your life and how will you do it?*

This time it is best to do the exercise from the perspective of your financial position as it is now. The question makes us aware of the reality that our lives are not infinite and our time on earth is limited. Five to ten years is a sufficiently long period to accomplish a lot but also a short enough period for us to realise that if there are things we want to do, we should not be putting them off.

Question 3: This time your doctor shocks you with the news that you have only one day left to live. Notice what feelings arise as you confront your very real mortality. Ask yourself: what did I miss? Who did I not get to be? What did I not get to do?

This question brings us face to face with our own mortality and relates directly to what we would want our lives to say about us. This can immediately help us realise what is important and what is less so, and focus our attention on what we should be doing.

The importance of these questions cannot be underestimated in the context of understanding what is truly important to you. Once these questions have been considered, mulled over and answered it is easier to look at your goals and aspirations. This is because you are putting them in the overall and wider context of your life.

Answering these three questions puts you in a good position to set out on a successful relationship with money. The answers start to give you real insight into what you would ideally do if you were able to cast off the limitations that hold you back. They put you in touch with what is really important to you and the part that money plays in all of this.

6.8 Set the foundations before you start work on your portfolio – the financial plan

Creating a *financial plan* is like laying the foundations of a building, with detailed architectural drawings showing how it is going to be built. Complete the plan before you start work on your portfolio. Failure to plan and pick the right tools will have predictable consequences – the most serious being that the aims of your plan will be missed entirely. More likely consequences are huge frustration and slow progress.

The financial plan is the map which, if you follow it correctly, will lead you to where you want to go: it helps make your dreams a reality, giving you a sense of achievement at the end of the process and the comfort of knowing that you are in control and financially organised.

Once you have set realistic goals, your adviser will help you work out where you are now in relation to these goals. They will get you to draw up a *balance sheet and income and expenditure account* (see Appendix 3) – these are really important, so you know where you are starting from.

Your adviser will also calculate your *'lifetime cash flow'* – usually to age 100. This is where all the information is pulled together and incorporated in your own plan for the future. Most people want to be outlived by their money rather than outliving their money themselves. This exercise shows you, based on the assumptions you make, whether this will be the case.

The beauty of this approach to creating a financial plan is that you now have a clear idea, based on the best assumptions that you can make, as to whether those things that you want to happen in your life are financially possible.

Knowledge is power, and you are now in a position to know how likely you are to achieve these goals, and, if you are not likely to do so, what has to change so you can achieve them. It is a genuine reality check-up and a possible wake-up call on your journey.

The road map is now in front of you and the route is laid out. You can alter it at any time, however, to suit a change in plan or circumstances. It is a wonderful feeling.

6.9 Conclusion

If we follow our natural biases and behavioural traits we reduce the likelihood of success, and sanity! Without a deep understanding of our natural and individual behavioural biases we cannot achieve a harmonious balance between life and money.

This chapter enables you to recognise the biases that as investors we are all prone to, outlining a strategy to explore and control them for a more successful investment experience – with the help of an expert guide.

If you can do this successfully, you will be relieved to hear that investment is actually a simple process. In the next chapter we explain this to give you clarity as you build your portfolio and start on your journey to financial peace of mind.

SECRET NO.

7

Investing is simple: *control the things you can control*

7.1 Introduction

Source: Dilbert[1]

In the early chapters of the book we highlighted the forces conspiring against you as an individual investor. We have argued that you cannot beat the market in the long term or control random events; when it comes to investment decisions, excitement should definitely be sought elsewhere.

Accepting these principles is truly liberating – freeing you up to focus on what you can control without being distracted by what you cannot. Investment then becomes a simple process designed to eliminate emotion and behavioural bias, working more as a science than an art to help you get to the destination you want.

There are three fundamental elements we can control when investing:

- *Risk* (the amount of risk it is appropriate for you take with your investments and how you manage that risk).

- *Structure* (how you effectively construct and manage your investment portfolio).

- *Costs and charges* (minimising tax leakage along the way).

These three fundamental drivers, when applied without emotion, are the starting point of what has been described as 'Winning the Loser's Game'.[2] Get these right and you tip the odds of investment success firmly in your favour.

We have touched on these driving principles in the previous chapters of the book: costs in Chapter 1, risk in Chapter 4 and structuring your portfolio in Chapter 5. In this chapter we pull these three elements together to give you a simple, practical process to follow when it comes to your investment strategy.

7.2 Risk and reward

Risk and reward are related, but we never know how they will play out in the short term. In the long term, however, we have a lot of evidence of how the various asset classes behave. Over time you will achieve a higher return for taking sensible extra risk with your investments. By paying attention to Chapter 4 you will be able to assess which risks are worth taking (and which are not).

With the knowledge from this book, and with the help of a good adviser, you will be able to work out what return you will need to achieve your goals and the appropriate asset allocation so that you do not take more risk than you can comfortably live with.

Understanding the different types of risk will ensure that your experience is not a roller-coaster ride, or, even worse, a smooth ride and then a collapse into the abyss, as experienced by investors with Bernie Madoff.

Managed properly through rebalancing, risk should be treated as an ally in achieving your investment goals. Only by accepting an appropriate level of risk will you be able to achieve your investment goals, but at times you may need reassurance.

Revisit this section should you begin to feel uncomfortable in a market downturn, and review the lessons that history has taught us in term of being patient with your investments.

7.3 Seven steps to an intelligently structured portfolio

Your financial plan will have laid out the big picture for you. You have considered your propensity for risk. It is now time to put together an intelligently constructed portfolio of investments to help achieve the short-, medium- and long-term goals you have set out in your plan.

There are seven clear steps you need to take here. You will have read about each of these in the previous chapters of the book, but here they are again, the building blocks of your investment portfolio set out as a practical plan for you to follow:

1) Asset allocation – equities and bonds

You know from Chapter 5 that asset allocation will determine most of the variability in the return on your investments. We advise you to invest widely in asset classes that research has shown provide a good risk-adjusted return, rather than in fashionable investments. We believe that you need to look no further than equities and bonds to do this.

Your adviser will help you to find the right split, depending on your risk tolerance – exploring how different scenarios have performed historically against model portfolios.

2) Equity allocation

Equities have proved over long periods of time to provide the highest returns compared to other asset classes. This return has come at a high price, however, in the form of periods of underperformance, demonstrating the relation of risk and reward.

Within the equity class higher returns have been found in certain classes of equities. Shares of smaller companies (small cap) have been found to have higher average returns than those of large companies (large cap), and shares in so-called 'value' companies provide investors with higher average returns than shares in 'growth' companies.

3) Diversification

Build a portfolio with a mixture of assets designed to give the highest possibility of achieving the expected return within your risk tolerance. Spread your investments globally across a number of different types of markets and you will fare a lot better than by betting on just one market.

4) Buy and hold

Trying to time the market (picking the best time to buy and sell) is potentially a recipe for disaster. Boring as it may sound, we recommend a buy-and-hold approach: stick with a strategy appropriate to your goals, risk tolerance, requirements for income and age.

Buy funds of equities rather than buying equities directly. In many jurisdictions you will garner a tax advantage by doing so. Your portfolio will be more diversified and therefore less risky. You will also save a lot of money:

- Who do you think gets the best deal when buying and selling equities? Is it a stockbroker managing 100 portfolios of £500,000 each, or is it the fund manager who works as part of an organisation with £100,000,000,000 under management?

The wise conclusion for nearly all investors is to use funds. We recommend a portfolio of exceptionally low-cost, well-engineered and well-executed smart index funds (as you will see in point 6 below).

Almost no marketing to individual clients is done by index management investment companies in the UK. They are focused on minimising costs, which is inconsistent with funding a large and expensive marketing campaign.

The few companies engaged in this area find it more efficient to sell to bigger, institutional investors such as big pension funds or a select few wealth managers. Smart indexing is well known in the institutional investing world, but little known to the individual investor.

One of the aims of writing this book is to bring institutional index-style investing to individual investors. It is the hidden gem of the investment world and a strategy that we strongly recommend.

(NB: The entire investment experience must be enjoyable. If you enjoy picking stocks and the high risk attached, do so. Recognise, however, that it is more speculative and enjoy it for what it is. *Concentrate on stock selection only if it gives you pleasure.* As a general rule, use funds rather than individual stocks.)

5) Appoint low-cost, passive fund managers

Use passive funds. Avoid getting carried away by the excitement of chasing managers and hot tips and ensure that your costs are minimised to improve your chance of a successful investment experience.

6) Use smart index funds (better than pure index funds)

We argue that a passive, low-fee, low-activity approach is likely to produce better returns in the medium and long term. One conventional way to achieve that aim is through buying a well-researched basket of index funds.

Now a basket of index funds will probably outperform a basket of active funds, but the authors of this book do not just buy index funds, nor do we recommend slavishly purchasing pure index funds for all asset classes. We suggest something slightly more refined, or smarter.

There are several things that make pure index funds unattractive. The biggest problem is their mechanical nature. Indices like the FTSE 100 are typically reconstituted every thirteen weeks or so. A fund that seeks to replicate the FTSE 100 could do so by buying and selling the same shares as make up the index. This means that, just as growing companies perhaps hit their peak and gain entry to the FTSE 100, our index fund starts buying them. The fund then owns them as long as the index, but when the company starts (relatively) declining or going through tough times our fund then sells the stock. But it seems a bit crazy to buy just off the peak and sell as the stock collapses. That does not fit with the rest of our advice.

The index reconstitution causes another problem. The FTSE 100 is essentially made up of the 100 largest firms listed on the London Stock Exchange. As the thirteen-week cycle comes around it is quite clear as the date gets closer which of those that at the last count were bubbling under at positions 101 to 110 are going to gain entry to the FTSE 100 index and which are going to be thrown out. Our index fund tracking fund *has* to buy the new entrants and *has* to sell the newly relegated. The market makers know this (remember, we think that the market is pretty clever) and so – guess what? – they increase the price of the assets the manager *has* to buy and decrease the price of the assets the manager *has* to sell.

What is the answer?

Intelligent and patient smart index investing. Fund managers we like do it as follows:

- Decide on an asset class – small European companies, for example.

- Do not slavishly follow a FTSE or MSCI index.

- Make your own definition of a small European company.

- Give yourself a little leeway. If a stock that meets your definition of a small European company becomes a medium-sized company and therefore fails to meet your definition, take your time selling it.

- Use all resources available to you to squeeze the best return out of the assets. Stay scientifically detached and remain indifferent regarding stock selection, but do not interpret this as a requirement to stick to an index.

- Own and trade assets in the most intelligent way possible – remain disciplined but flexible. Rigorous but not regimented. Smart not stupid.

So we use advanced or finessed passive funds, and we think you should too. Pure index funds are only a little different and will still generally beat retail active funds. But the best-of-breed solution is smart indexing.

7) Rebalancing

Without a structured maintenance programme the portfolio will quickly become functionally unsatisfactory. You will need to review it regularly to ensure it has the original risk parameters that you want.

Rebalancing is the planned maintenance of your investment portfolio. Regular rebalancing will ensure you stay within your pre-agreed risk tolerance. Sell high and buy low, as we discussed in Chapter 5.

7.4 Costs matter

Once you give up the effort involved in speculation, the success of long-term investing is largely a case of ensuring you get the highest return available from the underlying assets held in your portfolio. To ensure you keep more of your return, keep costs to a minimum. Look for ways to control the leakage from your investments caused by fees and taxation.

As we described in Chapter 1, there are many costs you need to be aware of when investing – commissions and other fees, sales charges and expenses. Always look into the fees – sometimes they are opaque; at other times purposely hidden.

How do you keep your costs to a minimum? *Choose to invest in passive not active funds.* As you learned in Chapter 3, active funds have much higher costs associated with their trading patterns, since each time they buy and sell to try to beat the market they incur costs and, in the UK, stamp duty on purchases.

In a 2007 article on investment research firm Morningstar's website, their director of fund research Christopher Trauslen wrote:

> *The issue should concern fund investors and their advisers – trading costs can often be so large as to swamp other more visible fees. Like all charges, they subtract directly from a fund's performance. Thus, if a fund's TER [Total Expense Ratio] is 1.70% and its trading costs are 1.70% per annum, your manager will have to outperform his*

benchmark by 3.4 percentage points per annum just to match the index – tall order even for a very good manager. In light of their importance, it seems rather shocking that the industry, or at least the FSA, isn't doing more to require funds to disclose trading costs in a meaningful manner to fund investors.[3]

Low-cost funds beat high cost funds: Morningstar recently examined five broad categories of equity and fixed-income funds over multiple periods beginning in 2005, 2006, 2007 and 2008 and ending in March 2010. Funds were sorted into quintiles based on expenses, and the performance of the cheapest funds was compared to that of the most expensive. Morningstar sells fund-ranking services, so their results are even more compelling. They computed total return for funds surviving through to March 2010 as well as a 'success ratio' measuring the percentage of the initial cohort that went on to survive and outperform their peers.

Unsurprisingly, cheap funds outperformed their expensive cousins.

Commenting on the results, Morningstar Director of Mutual Fund Research Russel Kinnel[4] observed:

In every single time period and data point tested, low-cost funds beat high-cost funds ... Investors should make expense ratios a primary test in fund selection. They are still the most dependable predictor of performance.

Costs matter: improve your chances of being a winner by keeping costs low.

7.5 Do not forget the tax implications

So, having arrived at a satisfactory asset allocation and managed costs effectively, you will need to consider the tax treatment of your investments.

The tax treatment of an investment is always important, as it will reduce the net return you receive: it is a cost and, like all costs, must be taken into account.

Let us look at an example:

- If the investment is in UK equities and is tax free, and the marginal rate of tax is 40% on income, then a tax-free investment might produce 7% per annum. A taxed investment might produce a return of 6% per annum.

- This small difference makes a big difference over the long term: £100,000 invested at 7% over 20 years will be worth £387,000. The same £100,000 invested at 6% over 20 years will be worth £322,000. That little 1% difference over 20 years makes approximately a massive 20% difference to the outcome!

Always arrange your investments in a tax-efficient manner. At the same time be sure not to let tax be the major cause of the investment. Many investments are set up purely to take advantage of the tax breaks that they give rather than the important consideration of the investment itself. If you put tax as the reason for the investment you will be taking a very specific and usually a highly concentrated risk.

We advise you to look carefully at the tax treatment of each available vehicle. Your adviser should help you here.

1. *Tax legislation changes regularly and dramatically.*
   Establishing an investment principally for tax reasons may make perfect sense this year. By next year the legislation may

have changed and the investment may be taxed in a very different way and be far less attractive from a tax perspective. If the investment is fundamentally sound and was chosen at a fundamental level because it fitted with your asset allocation decisions, then the revised tax treatment is a pain but no great disaster. If this is not the case you now own an investment that does not fit your investment plan, is not tax efficient, does not fit your asset allocation and may well be expensive.

2. *We have all been advising for years.* We regularly come across clients for whom tax considerations have been the overriding driver for investments. The client ends up with a portfolio that brings him or her no satisfaction at all.

   Typically the client will own a portfolio consisting of all sorts of small company investments (VCTs, EISs, BPR portfolios and so on) mixed in with some structured products designed to magically turn income into capital. The costs of running the portfolio will be extremely high and the client will be concerned about future legislative change, but worst of all the investments 'do not fit'.

   The reason the government offers tax relief on various investments is not because they feel generous. It is usually though not always because the investment has an inherent downside that means most investors would not purchase it.

Think carefully about whether the glossy tax wrapping covers a fundamentally duff investment. There are investments bought for tax reasons alone, and they are almost always bad news. We use all the above vehicles from time to time, but let the financial plan be the guide and driver rather than the tax situation.

7.6 Conclusion

Build your investment portfolio calmly. If you control the things you can control and try to ignore the things you cannot then investment becomes a simple process.

With the help of a good adviser you can control your emotions and recognise your natural human biases; control the amount of risk you take, the way you structure the building blocks of your portfolio, and the costs, taxes and fees this structure incurs. What you cannot control is what happens in the market – no one can. We firmly believe it is best not to try.

One of the drawbacks of this strategy is that you will not have any stories to tell about how you made a 'killing' by buying into a particular share or market at a particular time. If you have got this far in the book then hopefully you are more serious about your investment success than that.

Investment performance is what happens over the lifetime of your portfolio. When asked how long his ideal holding period for an investment is, investment guru Warren Buffett has been quoted as saying 'forever'. Like all successful investors he realises that time enables us to get the best from our investments.

Once you have your strategy, stick to it as closely as possible. Be patient and wait for your investments to deliver their long-term expected return. Make sure you keep within your agreed asset allocation through disciplined rebalancing.

Postscript

Keep calm when everyone else is panicking

If we cannot learn wisdom from experience it is hard to say where it is to be found.

George Washington[1]

Throughout this book we have been looking at how to get the results you want in your life with particular regard to the financial aspect. The investment process we have recommended is one that is bespoke to you, your life goals and your willingness to live with investment risk. If you follow our advice your journey should be much more comfortable than it would otherwise be.

Sometimes, however, things do go sadly awry, and it is at just such a time that you need to take a few deep breaths: do not panic, go back to your plan and see what changes need to be made. We have included this postscript to remind you to stay firm in the event of disaster or major dislocation.

Dealing with the downs

For the long-term investor one thing is certain: there will be times when you will seriously doubt your investment strategy. Even if you opt for a balanced portfolio, it is inevitable that there will be rocky patches.

As an example, take a balanced portfolio with, say, 50% in defensive investments like fixed interest and cash and 50% invested in shares. Your experience in holding this portfolio since 1 January 1970 will have looked like this:

- 37% of the time your investment will have been falling.
- 20% of the time your investment will have been recovering.
- 43% of the time your investment will have been rising.[2]

Your worst downside experience would have begun in January 1973 and over 24 months you would have lost a total of 27%, but your investments would have recovered just three months later. This shows how dangerous market timing is and how keeping your discipline is crucial to long-term success. The next-worst experience would have been from September 2000 for 29 months, when you would have lost 18.1% and taken 22 months to recover.

If you had taken a much higher risk and invested entirely in shares you would have lost approximately 49% from January 1973 over 21 months, taking 14 months to recover, and you would have lost 46% from September 2000 over 29 months, taking 37 months to recover. This shows how asset allocation can reduce the risk.

At times like this you will face a stiff test of your resolve.

Stay firm

Emotionally coping with the downs is part and parcel of investing: enter this world with a strong resolve and stay firm. History shows that the stock market has rewarded investors who can bear the risk of stocks and stay committed through various periods of performance. Just when things look really bad, very rapid turnarounds in market performance are the norm. The short-term risk is a necessary risk to take on if you are going to beat the biggest risk of all – inflation.

Do not panic: view market events and trends from a long-term perspective; stick to the disciplined approach to investment that we have outlined in the book. We will summarise this again for you in the book's conclusion.

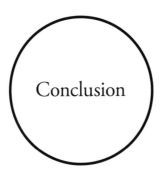

Conclusion

You can be a successful investor

We hope that we have shown you that, if you understand the secrets that the financial establishment has for so long kept to itself, it *is* possible to have a successful investment experience.

The most important message we want to get across is this: the secret to successful investment is not to try to forecast the markets – for you cannot beat the market in the long term – but instead to focus on the things you can control: concentrate on costs, properly diversify your risk, structure your portfolio the right way, stay disciplined, rebalance and – as important as all of that – seek out good independent financial advice.

Despite all the information you are bombarded with by the financial media and product manufacturers, we urge you to keep it simple. Do not confuse investing and speculating – it is not necessary to beat the market. Invest in a similar way to institutional investors and abide by an investment strategy that does not rely on forecasting if you want to meet your life goals.

If you follow the smart investment approach we outline you have a far better chance of:

■ Producing a return materially superior to that achieved by the average individual investor.

■ Experiencing a reassuring and interesting journey – in a vessel in which you have complete confidence. Courses and even itineraries may be altered from time to time, but the vessel is sound and time-tested and, despite the choppy water that all investors inevitably experience, you feel secure while on board.

■ Freeing up your time so you can concentrate on interesting and important stuff in your life.

steps to
investment success

Follow the 7 steps we outline in the book and you have
every chance of becoming a very successful investor.
We reiterate these steps here:

- **Step 1:** *Enlist the help of an expert financial guide* – a skilled,
  independent, fee-based adviser will keep you on purpose during
  your financial journey, particularly when things get tough.

- **Step 2:** *Understand your relationship with money.* Recognise
  and control your natural behavioural biases, which can
  sabotage a successful investment experience.

- **Step 3:** *Be clear on your life plans* and your short-, medium-
  and long-term financial goals.

- **Step 4:** *Think about your tolerance for risk* and understand the risks around investment to ensure a smooth ride.

- **Step 5:** Together with your financial adviser, *create a robust financial plan* to meet your goals, ensuring it is firmly grounded in the reality of your current financial situation.

- **Step 6:** *Design and build an intelligently constructed portfolio.* By following a sensibly devised plan whereby you spread your assets across a number of appropriate investments and keep the proportions allocated to those various investments in balance, you will give yourself the best possible chance of meeting your investment goals. As you will have read in Chapter 7, when building your portfolio concentrate on:

  - *Asset allocation:* Bonds and equities should be the main components of your portfolio – nothing else will give you the same portfolio benefits, at a low cost, and in a reliable manner.

  - *Equity allocation:* By holding a larger portion of small-cap and value equities in a portfolio, you will increase the potential to earn higher returns for the additional risk taken. *Remember: value beats growth and small beats large.*

  - *Diversify:* Do not put all your eggs in one basket. Spread your investments globally across a number of different types of markets and you will fare a lot better than by betting on just one market.

  - *Buy and hold smart index-based funds:* Buy funds of equities rather than buying equities directly. We recommend a portfolio of exceptionally low-cost, well-engineered and well-executed smart index funds.

  - *Appoint low-cost, passive fund managers:* Use passive funds and ensure that your costs are minimised to improve your chance of a successful investment experience.

– *Rebalance:* Use a pre-agreed rebalancing strategy to maintain your agreed risk level.

■ **Step 7:** *Keep the discipline;* understand your investments and the return drivers and be patient. Wait for your investments to deliver their long-term expected return while making sure that you keep within your agreed asset allocation and the discipline of rebalancing.

Take action

Take these 7 steps and feel the freedom of having real understanding and confidence around money.

Having read this book, you may ask yourself why this approach is not more prevalent among private investors. If you were offered an investment strategy that was reassuring, not time consuming, was likely to produce the return you needed to achieve your important goals, had stood the test of time and was supported by Nobel laureates and some of the most famous investors on the planet, WHY WOULD YOU NOT GIVE IT A GO?

What is the catch, you may ask? There are two:

■ *Embracing our theories involves ditching sacred cows.* That can be very, very hard.

■ *It is not sexy or instant.* And in our culture many people often want sexy and instant.

If you are willing to deal with a way of looking at money that politely and scientifically questions what might be your existing beliefs; if you are willing to embrace a style of investing that sees simplicity as a virtue; if you can invest money knowing *for certain* that you will lose money from time to time, but have confidence in the model and your adviser to deliver in the long term … then you can open the door to an investment experience that is vastly superior to what most private investors currently suffer.

Our book gives you various techniques and structures to use, coupled with some advice that other people have found helpful. To keep it short we have skated over some detail. But the keys to opening the door to a satisfying investment experience are all contained in the text.

We do sincerely hope that you will use some of the keys and we thank you sincerely for reading our book.

Simon Brown
Ben Sherwood
Richard Stott
Bruce Wilson
2011

Appendix

Historical best and worst returns for the investment portfolios detailed in Chapter 5

We have included this appendix to give you an idea of what it would feel like to hold our recommended index-based portfolios over one, three, five, ten, fifteen and twenty years, to show you a full range of the best and worst returns that you can expect.

In the chart you will see that:

- The highest-risk investment (equity) provided the highest average return over every time period, but had a –34.31% worst return over a twelve-month period.

- By investing in a moderate-risk profile, about 1% or less of return per annum is given up in the long term, but the worst return over a one-year period is just –11.34%.

This loss in return sounds quite small, but over a twenty-year period compound interest does its magic: your overall return would have been 783% from the equity portfolio and 524% from the moderate risk-portfolio.

The question is: do you need to take this additional risk? Or more importantly, would you stay the course if you saw the value of your portfolio decline by 34% over a twelve-month period?

As the chart shows, by diversifying your investments you can reduce your overall risk level significantly and still earn a very attractive return from your portfolio.

Best/ Worst Return

Monthly: 01/1988 - 02/2011; Default Currency: GBP

Annualized Average Rolling Return	1 Year		3 Years		5 Years		10 Years		15 Years		20 Years	
Equity	10.70%		8.78%		9.23%		8.27%		8.44%		8.51%	
Best Return (%)	64.29%	(9/1992)	28.37%	(2/1991)	20.35%	(9/1992)	15.97%	(10/1990)	11.68%	(9/1992)	10.97%	(1/1988)
Worst Return (%)	-34.31%	(11/2007)	-14.91%	(4/2000)	-4.62%	(4/1998)	1.36%	(3/1999)	3.83%	(9/1992)	6.58%	(3/1989)
Aggressive	9.89%		8.54%		8.87%		8.07%		8.21%		8.38%	
Best Return (%)	50.90%	(9/1992)	24.47%	(2/1991)	17.50%	(9/1992)	14.31%	(10/1990)	10.66%	(2/1991)	10.46%	(1/1988)
Worst Return (%)	-26.72%	(11/2007)	-10.94%	(4/2000)	-2.41%	(4/1998)	2.41%	(3/1999)	4.40%	(3/1994)	6.94%	(3/1989)
Normal	9.30%		8.38%		8.66%		8.04%		8.15%		8.29%	
Best Return (%)	41.64%	(9/1992)	20.95%	(2/1991)	15.59%	(1/1989)	13.12%	(4/1988)	10.05%	(2/1991)	10.12%	(1/1988)
Worst Return (%)	-21.19%	(3/2008)	-6.08%	(4/2000)	-0.14%	(4/1998)	3.40%	(3/1999)	4.87%	(3/1994)	7.24%	(3/1989)
Moderate	8.24%		7.72%		7.77%		7.29%		7.36%		7.66%	
Best Return (%)	27.02%	(9/1992)	16.64%	(2/1991)	14.24%	(1/1989)	11.77%	(4/1988)	8.81%	(1/1988)	9.04%	(1/1988)
Worst Return (%)	-11.34%	(3/2008)	-3.05%	(4/2000)	1.68%	(4/1998)	3.94%	(4/1999)	5.12%	(3/1994)	7.08%	(7/1990)
Conservative	7.39%		7.14%		7.04%		6.71%		6.75%		7.09%	
Best Return (%)	19.28%	(1/1989)	14.77%	(6/1988)	13.17%	(1/1989)	10.53%	(4/1988)	8.45%	(1/1988)	8.15%	(1/1988)
Worst Return (%)	-3.68%	(3/2008)	0.88%	(4/2000)	3.57%	(4/1998)	4.06%	(9/2000)	5.28%	(3/1994)	6.34%	(3/1991)
Fixed	6.53%		6.45%		6.20%		6.02%		6.01%		6.38%	
Best Return (%)	15.93%	(10/1989)	14.33%	(8/1988)	12.43%	(1/1988)	9.21%	(1/1988)	7.97%	(1/1988)	7.14%	(1/1988)
Worst Return (%)	0.41%	(6/2009)	1.66%	(3/2008)	3.11%	(3/2006)	3.73%	(3/2001)	4.57%	(3/1996)	5.30%	(3/1991)

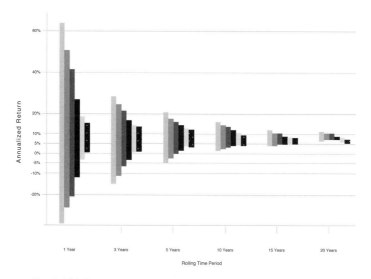

Please see Standardized Performance Data and Disclosures (available at the end of this presentation) for information on performance, investment objectives, risks, fees and expenses of Dimensional funds. Performance data represents past performance. Past performance is no guarantee of future results and current performance may be higher or lower than the performance shown. Please read the prospectus carefully before investing, available by calling Dimensional on 020 7016 4500 or at www.dfauk.com.

Appendix

Selection criteria – a list of questions to ask a potential financial adviser

Below are some valuable questions to ask an adviser about their investment philosophy before you decide to work with them:

A) Questions about investing

1. How will the way you invest my money change as your forecasts for financial markets change?

If the answer is anything other than 'we do not and cannot forecast markets', then you need go no farther with your questions!

2. Can I see your investment policy statement?

Detailed and simplified versions should be available to cater for different sorts of clients. A policy statement should be available, otherwise you are investing your money in the unknown and possibly subjecting it to one individual's own market view at the time. Their policy statement should contain an emphasis on asset allocation, low-cost passive and/or index funds, discipline rebalancing, and benchmarking to monitor performance. Look for details on how new money will be invested and how withdrawals will be taken.

3. What is the typical Annual Management Charge (AMC) and Total Expense Ratio (TER) for a balanced portfolio?

The AMC should be in the order of 0.4%. Any adviser's fees will be in addition to this cost. The Total Expense Ratio is an estimate of the total annual running expense of a fund, including the AMC and fixed costs such as administration, legal audit and custody fees. It does not include the cost of dealing and should be in the order of 0.5%.

4. How do you invest your money?

This should be invested according to the same strategy as they recommend to you. Any other answer and they do not practise what they preach.

B) Questions to ask concerning advice process and service

There are many well-qualified advisers who still think investment is a skill not a process, and it is better to weed those out first. The following questions are more about the adviser's process and client service:

1. Can I see the process you go through to take on a new client?

This should provide a step-by-step guide to each stage of the process and should include a minimum of three meetings before any money is invested.

2. How do you assess my attitude to investment risk and how does this translate into the portfolio you recommend?

Most good advisers use detailed risk profile questionnaires with some fifty questions on them to ensure they are robust. The adviser should be clear that this is just to give an indication of your natural tolerance to risk: merely the starting point for a discussion on risk.

The eventual risk you take will be informed by the return required for you to achieve your goals, which will be calculated by the cash flow model.

Very often there is a mismatch between the risk you are prepared to take and the risk you need to take, and this should be openly discussed as a core function of the financial process.

3. How will my plan be reviewed?

This should be at least annually but may be half-yearly. Some advisers do an investment review once a year and a separate financial planning and/or life planning review also once a year with the two six months apart. You should expect to be contacted before the review meeting for updated financial information, such as changes to income or expenditure or cash in the bank. You should also be given the opportunity to forewarn the adviser of any scenarios you may wish to discuss (such as downsizing, buying a second home, going on a cruise, helping children/grandchildren, changing job, etc.) so that when you meet your adviser your financial plan and cash flow are up to date and the implications of any proposed changes ready to be discussed.

You should be clear how the performance of your investments will be judged each year. Find out when rebalancing will occur.

All meetings should have a formal agenda and minutes taken with follow-up action points to keep everything on track.

You can download these questions from our website,
www.7secretsofmoney.co.uk

Appendix

Drawing up your income and expenditure accounts and a net worth statement

Before you and your chosen adviser create your financial plan you will need to draw up an income and expenditure account and a net worth statement.

This is a really important exercise so you know where you are starting from and where you are in relation to your goals.

Income account

The income statement is for most of us much easier to do as we have only one or two items of income. It is however important that you capture all of your income.

Draw up your income account listing your income in all its forms.

Income Record

Salary/wages	
Self employment net earnings	
Pension	
Dividends	
Interest	
Rent	
Trust	
Royalties	
Other	
GROSS INCOME =	

We suggest that you do this on a gross annual basis rather than monthly, as income such as dividends, interest, trust and royalties are not always received each month. All your income will need to be shown on your annual tax return.

The final piece in the income jigsaw is any tax and national insurance that you will need to pay. This should be deducted from your gross income. This will give you your net income after tax. It is this figure that you have available to spend and save to help you in delivering your life and financial goals.

Expenditure account

Here is a comprehensive table on which to record your expenditure:

House	Mortgage interest and capital repayment	
	Rent	
	Building contents insurance	
	Council tax	
	Decoration and maintenance	
	Gardening	
	TV licence	
Utilities	Electricity	
	Gas	
	Water	
	Telephones and broadband	
	Solid fuel	
Housekeeping	Food	
	Alcohol	
	Home entertainment	
	Media rental	
Motor	Fuel	
	Servicing	
	Insurance	
	Road tax	
	RAC/AA membership	
	Replacement allowance	
Travel and leisure	Rail and bus fares	

	Holidays	
	Club subscriptions	
	Entertainment	
	Tobacco	
	Books, magazines, newspapers	
	Sports/hobbies	
	Music and films	
Personal	Clothing	
	Presents	
	Pocket money and allowances	
	Charitable donations	
	Education	
	Maintenance or alimony	
	Loan/finance interest and charges	
Savings and personal insurance	Current investments	
	Pensions	
	ISAs	
	Life assurance	
	Income protection	
	Critical illness	
	Savings for repayment of mortgage	
	Other savings	

Net worth statement / balance sheet

You will probably be familiar with the term 'balance sheet' as it relates to companies and businesses. It is simply a statement at a specific date of all the assets and liabilities that the company has at that date, to show the net worth of the company.

When doing this for yourself, rather than call it a balance sheet it is simpler to call it a 'net worth statement', because it will show your net worth at a specific date.

To help you complete your net worth statement we have listed below the most common items, both assets and liabilities, that you may have.

Your net worth will be positive if your assets are greater than your liabilities and negative if your liabilities are greater than your assets.

Asset record

Property:	
Home	
Investment properties	
Investments:	
Personal equity plans	
Individual savings accounts	
Stocks and shares	
Unit and investment trusts	
Venture capital trusts	
Enterprise investment schemes	
Bonds/gilts	
Private equity	
Pensions:	
Current market or transfer value	

Cash:	
Bank	
Building societies	
Other	
Other assets:	
Cars	
House contents	
Antiques	
Other	
TOTAL ASSETS =	

Liability record

Mortgages	
Bank loans	
Credit cards	
Car loan	
Education loans	
Personal debts	
Tax	
Other	
TOTAL LIABILITIES =	

YOUR NET WORTH (ASSETS – LIABILITIES)	£ ....

You can download these forms from our website,
www.7secretsofmoney.co.uk

Appendix

This chart, overleaf, shows the pattern of returns from different sizes of company in markets around the world, as described in Chapter 5, page 83

Size and Value Effects Are Strong around the World

Annual Index Data

Percent per Annum in £

Annualised Compound Returns

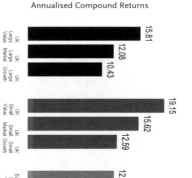

	UK Large Capitalisation Stocks (£) 1956–2009		
	UK Large Value Market	UK Large Market	UK Large Growth
	15.81	12.08	10.43

	UK Small Capitalisation Stocks (£) 1956–2009		
	UK Small Value Market	UK Small Market	UK Small Growth
	19.15	15.62	12.59

	Europe ex UK Large Capitalisation Stocks (€) 1981–2009		
	Europe Large Value Market	Europe Large Market	Europe Large Growth
	12.15	9.53	8.15

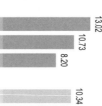

	Europe ex UK Small Capitalisation Stocks (€) 1981–2009		
	Europe Small Value Market	Europe Small Market	Europe Small Growth
	13.02	10.73	8.20

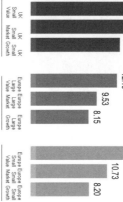

	US Large Capitalisation Stocks ($) 1927–2009		
	US Large Value	S&P 500 Index	US Large Growth
	10.34	9.79	8.95

	US Small Capitalisation Stocks ($) 1927–2009		
	US Small Value	CRSP 6-10 Index	US Small Growth
	13.59	11.49	8.72

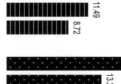

	Emerging Markets Capitalisation Stocks ($) 1989–2009		
	Emg Markets Value	Emg Markets "Market"	Emg Markets Growth
	17.97	13.30	10.81

Standard Deviation (%)

	UK Large Value	UK Large Market	UK Large Growth	UK Small Value	UK Small Market	UK Small Growth	Europe Large Value	Europe Large Market	Europe Large Growth	Europe Small Value	Europe Small Market	Europe Small Growth	US Large Value	S&P 500	US Large Growth	US Small Value	CRSP 6-10	US Small Growth	Emg Markets Value	Emg Markets Market	Emg Markets Growth
	32.08	28.60	26.29	31.81	30.34	30.83	27.22	23.29	25.76	26.10	24.80	27.51	27.17	20.63	22.06	35.30	31.09	34.20	43.04	37.29	35.70

Reproduced by kind permission of Dimensional.

Recommended reading

For those who want to delve deeper into the subject, we have each noted a favourite book on finance and investing.

Simon Brown recommends:

It's Not about the Money by Brent Kessel. This book will help you understand the 'Wanting Mind', identify your 'Financial Archetype' and provides information and resources as well as exercises and meditations to inspire a fresh approach to your relationship with money: an approach that will change your life from the inside out. Visit www.brentkessel.com for a preview of the book's contents or take the Financial Archetype test to start the journey of self-discovery.

It's Not about the Money: Unlock Your Money Type to Achieve Spiritual and Financial Abundance, HarperOne, 2008

Ben Sherwood *recommends:*

The Intelligent Investor by Benjamin Graham. Many of
the basic ideas in this book are contained in his earlier
publication, *Security Analysis*. These books were written
in the 1930s and 1940s. The detail of the measures needs
revision for the 21st century but the principles are as relevant
now as they were then. Yes, it can be heavy going (if that
sounds daunting, try *The Undercover Economist* by Tim
Harford), but before you decide not to bother with Graham,
do not forget what Warren Buffett said about his book: 'the
best book about investment ever written'.

The Intelligent Investor, first published 1949, 4th revision with
Jason Zweig, HarperCollins, 2003

Richard Stott *recommends:*

Smarter Investing by Tim Hale. If you want to explore the
investment philosophies and ideas we have discussed, this is
an excellent book to deepen your knowledge. Written by one
of the most knowledgeable independent experts in the UK,
it brings together research from many different sources and
presents the reader with concrete ideas and recommendations
for a successful investment experience.

Smarter Investing: Simpler Decisions for Better Results, 2nd edition,
FT Prentice Hall, 2009

*Bruce **Wilson*** *recommends:*

The Seven Stages of Money Maturity by George Kinder. George is considered by many to be the founding father of the life planning movement. In this book he expounds his theory that our relationship to money is fundamental to our investment and financial behaviour, and that it all starts with our earliest memories around money. His book charts the journey we can take from innocence and pain to understanding and wisdom, all in the context of making money work in our lives.

The Seven Stages of Money Maturity: Understanding the Spirit and Value of Money in your Life, Dell Publishing, 2000

About the
authors

The authors of this book are four highly respected finance professionals – each running their own independent firm. All share a common belief in how the market works and how individuals should approach money and investment. They have collaborated to provide this clear guide to protecting and growing your money.

Simon Brown
www.bphwealth.co.uk

Simon is a partner at BPH Wealth Management and has 23 years' experience advising clients. He is the first certified wealth mentor in the UK, working closely with 35 families based in the UK and overseas and acting as the investment counsellor to several trustee bodies. He enjoys learning from best business and wealth management practice around the world and implementing the latest thinking and methods in his work.

Simon is an Associate of the Chartered Insurance Institute, a Chartered Financial Planner, a Certified Financial Planner and

Certified Wealth Mentor. Simon has studied Practical Philosophy for fifteen years and practises regular meditation. He is actively involved in Strategic Coach, a powerful coaching programme for business owners.

Simon aims to liberate, guide and empower as many people as possible to reach their potential through greater self-knowledge and understanding. He believes that helping to provide clarity of life purpose and improving understanding of behaviour around money are key to developing the confidence required to plan and live a quality life.

Contact Simon –
T: 01582 466738; E: simon.brown@bphwealth.co.uk

Ben Sherwood
www.satisuk.com

Ben has worked in the financial services industry since 1987. He is a partner in the chartered accountancy firm Hillier Hopkins LLP and director of Satis Asset Management Ltd, where he advises a select group of clients on both investment consultancy and tax planning. Ben's specialism is dealing with the particular issues faced by clients between the ages of 55 and 100. He is fascinated by the investment world and works with experts who can help with taxation and other financial matters.

Ben holds various qualifications and is both a Chartered Financial Planner and a Certified Financial Planner.

He strongly believes that investment planning need not be complicated. His primary role is as sounding board, devil's advocate and experienced guide.

Contact Ben –
T: 0207 004 7121; E: ben.sherwood@satisuk.com

Richard Stott
www.connectum.no

Richard is a founding partner and Chief Investment Officer at Connectum Capital Management AS, based in Norway. He has worked in the investment industry ever since leaving further education and has worked extensively with individual investors, entrepreneurs, families, trusts and foundations around the world.

After many years working for large institutions and some of the best-known names in the industry, becoming a founder partner in a wealth management business led Richard to search out the best in global wealth management practices. He is dedicated to furthering investor education and awareness both in Norway, where he lives and runs his business, and around the world, where he and his business partners look after clients in five different time zones.

Richard is a member of the Chartered Financial Analysts Institute, a member of the Norwegian Financial Analysts Association, a Trust and Estate Practitioner, and a member of the Institute of Financial Planning.

Richard wants to show people that with a little bit of work and research, successful investing can be fairly uncomplicated and relatively inexpensive.

Contact Richard –
T: +47 90 72 27 80;
E: richard.stott@connectum.no
Richard on Twitter: www.twitter.com/stotty67
Richard's personal blog: richardstott.blogspot.com

Bruce Wilson
www.helmgodfrey.com

From 1999 to 2010 Bruce was the founding managing director of Helm Godfrey Partners, a firm of independent financial advisers based in the city of London. He is now a director, shareholder and client adviser. Under Bruce's management Helm won two prestigious awards – *Money Marketing*'s IFA of the year and *Financial Adviser*'s Large IFA of the year for 2008.

Bruce is currently vice-president of the Institute of Financial Planning, of which he is a Fellow. He is a Certified Financial Planner (CFP), a Registered Life Planner (RLP) and a chartered accountant. He is also a founder member of Project Eve – an association of Registered Life Planners dedicated to promoting the integrity of financial planning with life planning.

As a leading advocate of life planning, Bruce is committed to forging a new and radically client-focused approach that puts the client back at the centre of the financial planning process.

Contact Bruce –
T: 020 7614 1000;
E: bruce@helmgodfrey.com

You can find out more about the authors, their companies and further articles and resources on the topics covered in this book at **www.7secretsofmoney.co.uk**.

Acknowledgements

We are indebted to George Kinder for the thoughtful foreword and to our book reviewers, Tim Hale, Paul Bradshaw, Mark Baldry and Janice Trebble. All have many time commitments of their own but nevertheless showed remarkable generosity, and we are very grateful to them.

We would like to thank our clients who have been kind enough to entrust their financial futures to us. We can only hope that they have found and will continue to find our journey together beneficial. We continue to value not only their business but also the knowledge we have gained from dealing with them and, in many cases, the friendships formed.

We would like to express our thanks to Sonja Jefferson of Valuable Content, without whom this book would still be just an idea. Sonja project-managed and edited the book and demonstrated remarkable patience with all of us and the inevitable frustrations of dealing with four busy people working on one project. Sonja was able to help distil our ideas into a coherent form and find common ground when we had disparate views.

Eli Barbary of Barbary Solutions did a very professional job of gaining permission for all the quotes and references in the book and managed to coordinate four diaries to arrange regular telephone conferences and meetings.

Daniel Penfold has done a brilliant job with the book design and again found common ground very quickly between us, making this part of the process painless.

Paul Forty and his team turned our draft into a fully copy-edited and proofread manuscript, and he project-managed the whole pre- and post-production process for us which, combined with Daniel's design, gave us the finished article, of which we are immensely proud.

A final thank-you goes to our families and partners for putting up with our burning the midnight oil and being somewhat preoccupied during the writing process.

Notes and references

Epigraph

1. Friedrich August von Hayek (8 May 1899–23 March 1992) was an Austrian economist and philosopher. He won the Nobel Prize in Economics with Swedish economist Gunnar Myrdal in 1974 for his work on the theory of money and economic fluctuations. The source of this quote is unknown.

Introduction

1. Leo Tolstoy (9 September 1828–20 November 1910) was a Russian novelist whose works include *War and Peace* and *Anna Karenina*. The source of this quote is unknown.

Secret no. 1

1. Dilbert cartoon strip reproduced with permission from the Dilbert series by Scott Adams (this strip published 21 August 2008). The original version can be found at http://dilbert.com/strips/comic/2009-08-21

2. In 2013 in America, Dalbar updated the study known as the Quantitative Analysis of Investor Behaviour (QAIB) – www.qaib.com shows the most recent version.

3. In 2007 Lukas Schneider wrote a thesis entitled 'Are UK fund investors achieving fund rates of return? An examination of the differences between UK fund returns and UK investors' returns'. It can be found at www.ebisgroup.org under the heading 'Passive vs. Active Management'.

4. Bernard Madoff was the owner of Bernard L Madoff Investment Securities as well as a separate hedge fund business. In 2008 Madoff engineered a fraud of great magnitude, using his two businesses, by using money from new investors to pay previous investors. Among the victims were some of the world's largest banks, including Santander, HSBC and the Royal Bank of Scotland. The total amount of money lost was $65 billion (£40 billion). Madoff was sentenced to 150 years.

5. From 'Fund Management 2010' by TheCityUK Research Centre, www.thecityuk.com.

6. International Financial Services London (IFSL) is an independent membership body, promoting the UK financial and related professional services industry. Web: www.ifsl.org.uk; Tel.: 0207 776 8970; Email: info@thecityuk.com; Address: 65a Basinghall Street, London EC2V 5DZ.

7. You can find more on 'active' investment management strategies in Chapter 3 of the book.

8. Academic studies proving the premise that active management reduces net returns: K. James, 'The price of retail investing in the UK', Occasional Paper no. 6, Financial Services Authority, 2000; Mark M. Carhart, 'On persistence in mutual fund performance', FSA Occasional Paper 6 , Kepos Capital LP; *Journal of finance*, 52(1), March 1997.

9. John Bogle founded the Vanguard Group in 1974 – www.vanguard.com – now one of the largest fund management companies in the world. He likens the stock market to a casino and uses the term 'croupiers' in several of his publications, including the excellent *The Little Book of Common Sense Investing*, published by Wiley, 111 River Street, Hoboken, NJ 07030-5774, USA; www.wiley.com; ISBN: 0470 102 101.

10. We refer to FSA Occasional Paper 6 by Kevin R. James, 'The price of retail investing', February 2000, Section 2.3. This can be found at http://www.fsa.gov.uk/pubs/occpapers/op06.pdf.

11. NB: Not all the 3.7% flows to the fund manager or broker; as mentioned above, the UK government gets some and various other parties in the financial services food chain also receive some income.

12. Dalbar, op. cit., www.qaib.com.

13. Schneider, op. cit., www.ebisgroup.org.

Secret no. 2

1. Dalbar, op. cit., www.qaib.com.

2. 'Super Duper Fund' is an entirely fictitious company to illustrate the point – the company name is made up but the examples are based on the actions of real companies.

3. Note to mathematicians: yes we are aware that there are some assumptions here regarding exactly when in years 3 and 4 clients invested, and how the fund return was delivered, and whether all investors invested the same monetary amount. These are all valid points. Our observations are also valid. Far too often fund management groups advertise claims based on fund performance that only a small number of investors have actually enjoyed. We can move from here to a discussion of time-weighted versus

money-weighted returns. If you are interested in this detail, do drop the authors a line.

4. Press Complaints Commission, Halton House, 20–23 Holborn, London EC1N 2JD; Tel.: 0207 831 0022; Web: www.pcc.org.uk; Email: complaints@pcc.org.uk.

5. Bimonthly American publication *Fortune* magazine was founded by Henry Luce in 1930. 'Confessions of a former mutual funds reporter' was published in the April 1999 issue by an anonymous author.

6. For more on 'buy and hold' strategies, see Chapter 7, section 3, point 4.

Secret no. 3

1. Daniel Kahneman (born 5 March 1934) is the Professor of Psychology and Public Affairs at Princeton University. He won the 2002 Nobel Memorial Prize for Economics for his work on Prospect Theory. Quote reproduced by kind permission of the author.

2. The Efficient Market Hypothesis (EMH) in investment terms explains why it is unlikely to be possible to beat the market more often than might be expected by chance. The EMH was developed in the second half of the twentieth century. Professor Eugene Fama of the Chicago Business School has been responsible for developing the EMH, and it was he who first defined the terms and hypothesis in the 1960s.

There are various versions of the hypothesis but the essential point is that markets price investments fairly (for investment purposes).

EMH has become controversial in some quarters because of recent market turmoil. The authors of this book, however, see nothing inconsistent with volatile markets and EMH. Indeed, as information becomes available we would expect prices to move about. EMH is not an explanation for or an antidote against market volatility.

The explanation on the Dimensional Fund Advisors' site, www.dimensional.com, is excellent:

'The Efficient Market Hypothesis says that market prices are fair: they fully reflect all available information. This does not mean that prices are perfect; some prices may be too high and some too low, but there is no reliable way to tell. In an efficient market, investors cannot expect to earn above-average profits without assuming above-average risks. Market efficiency does not suggest that investors can't "win." Over any period of time, some investors will beat the market, but the number of investors who do so will be no greater than expected by chance.'

3. C. Blake, E. J. Elton and M. J. Gruber, 'The performance of bond mutual funds', *Journal of Business*, 1993, 66(3): 371–403.

4. E. J. Elton, M. J. Gruber, S. Das and M. Hlavka, 'Efficiency with costly information: a reinterpretation of evidence from managed portfolios', *Review of Financial Studies*, 1993, 6: 1–22.

5. Barras, Scaillet and Wermers, 'False discoveries in mutual fund performance: measuring luck in estimated alphas', Research Paper Series no. 08–18, Swiss Finance Institute, 2008.

6. Michael C. Jensen (born 30 November 1939) is an American economist working in the field of financial economics. He is currently the MD of Monitor Group (a strategy consulting firm) and Professor of Business Administration, Emeritus, at Harvard University. The study we refer to is entitled 'The performance of mutual funds in the period 1945–1964', which can be found at http://www.edge-fund.com/Jens67.pdf.

7. Mark Carhart is a former co-head of Goldman Sachs Asset Management's quantitative investing group. The study referenced here is 'On persistence in mutual fund performance', *Journal of Finance*, March 1997, 52(1), which can be found at http://stuwww.uvt.nl/fat/files/library/ Carhart,%20Mark%20M.%20-%20On%20Persistence%20 in%20Mutual%20Fund%20Performance%20(1997).pdf.

8. Source: Carhart, op. cit. Reproduced by kind permission of Dimensional.

9. William F. Sharpe, 'The arithmetic of active management', *Financial Analysts' Journal*, January/February 1991, 47(1): 7–9. The full article can be found at http://www.stanford. edu/~wfsharpe/art/active/active.htm.

10. Warren Buffett, in the Chairman's Letter, 1996 Berkshire Hathaway Corp. Annual Report.

11. The late Merton Miller, co-recipient of the 1990 Nobel Prize in Economic Sciences and former member of the DFA board of directors, in Peter J. Tanous, *Investment Gurus*, New York Institute of Finance, Paramus, NJ, 1997, pp. 225–6.

Secret no. 4

1. *Dragon's Den* is a popular BBC UK television show in which entrepreneurs pitch their business ideas in hope of investment; www.bbc.co.uk/dragonsden.

2. Active managers seek to beat the market through stock selection and market timing. They generally charge higher fees than passive managers as compensation for their perceived 'skill'. These fees can inflict a significant penalty on net investment returns and terminal wealth, as this graph demonstrates for various cost levels. Table reproduced by kind permission of Dimensional.

Secret no. 5

1. Dilbert cartoon strip reproduced with permission from the Dilbert series by Scott Adams (this strip published 14 March 2007). The original version can be found at http://dilbert.com/strips/comic/2007-03-14.

2. G. P. Brinson, L. Randolph Hood and G. L. Beebower, 'Determinants of portfolio performance', *Financial Analysts Journal*, July/August 1986 (revised 1991); Ibbotson and Kaplan, 'Does asset allocation policy explain 40, 90, or 100 percent of performance', *Financial Analysts Journal,* January/February 2000.

3. Roger Gibson, *Asset Allocation*, 4th edn, McGraw-Hill, 2007, ISBN-10: 0071478094, ISBN-13: 978-0071478090.

4. E. Dimson, P. Marsh and M. Staunton, *Millennium Book II: 101 Years of Investment Returns,* ABN AMRO and London Business School, 2001. Reproduced by kind permission of Dimensional.

5. Reproduced by kind permission of Dimensional.

6. One-time president of the American Finance Association and professor emeritus of Stanford University, William F. Sharpe (born 16 June 1934) is the winner of the 1990 Nobel Memorial Prize in Economic Sciences for his role in developing the Capital Asset Pricing Model. Among his work is the book *Portfolio Theory and Capital Markets*, McGraw-Hill, 1970, ISBN: 0071353208.

7. E. F. Fama and K. R. French, 'Common risk factors in the returns on stock and bonds', *Journal of Financial Economics*, 1993, 33: 3–56.

8. FTSE data courtesy of FTSE. MSCI data copyright MSCI 2010. All rights reserved. Reproduced by kind permission of Dimensional.

9. Professor Eugene Fama (born 14 February 1939) is an American economist. He is known for his work on portfolio theory and asset pricing. He is currently Professor of Finance at the University of Chicago Booth School of Business.

Professor Kenneth French (born 10 March 1954) is also an American economist. He is most famous for his work with Eugene Fama on asset pricing. He is currently Professor of Finance at Tuck School of Business, Dartmouth College.

10. Value Index, 1955–December 1993: data provided by the London Business School; 1994–present simulated by Dimensional from Bloomberg securities data. Small Cap Index, 1970–June 1981: Hoare Govett Smaller Companies Index; July 1981–December 1993 simulated by Dimensional from Style Research securities data; 1994–present simulated by Dimensional from Bloomberg securities data. Large Cap Index is the FTSE All-Share Index published with the permission of FTSE. T-Bills, 1955–1974: UK Three-Month Bills provided by the London Share Price Database; 1975–present: UK One-Month T-Bills provided by the *Financial Times*. Inflation is the UK Retail Price Index provided by the Office for National Statistics.

11. J. Tobin, 'Liquidity preference as behaviour towards risk', *Review of Economic Studies*, February 1958, 67.

12. All statistics reproduced by kind permission of Dimensional.

Secret no. 6

1. Quote reproduced by kind permission of DNA Behaviour International, Financial DNA Resources, www.financialdna.com.

2. Source: Dalbar, Inc., Quantitative Analysis of Investor Behaviour, July 2008. This computed the 'average stock fund investor' returns by using industry cash flow reports from the Investment Company Institute. The 'average stock fund' return figures represent the average return for all funds listed in Lipper's US Diversified Equity fund classification model.

3. Sir Isaac Newton (4 January 1643–31 March 1727), most well known for discovering gravity, was one of the most influential scientists in history. This quote first appears in Henry Richard Fox Bourne, *The Romance of Trade*, 1876, as 'I can calculate the motions of erratic stars, but not the madness of the multitude' (it was supposedly Newton's opinion on the consequences of the South Sea Bubble).

4. A brief history of behavioural finance: 35 years ago a young finance academic, Richard Thaler, and a friend were contemplating driving across Rochester, New York, in a blinding snowstorm to see a basketball game. They wisely decided not to, but Thaler wondered whether they would have made a different decision if they had already bought tickets, which of course should make no difference to the risk assessment of driving in a snowstorm.

   At about the same time, two psychologists, Daniel Kahneman and Amos Tversky, published a landmark paper in a prestigious science journal in which they outlined the basic errors in human judgement.

   Thaler and his followers were able to extend Kahneman and Tversky's work to economics and helped found the new field of behavioural finance. Tversky died in 1996, but six years later Kahneman was awarded the Nobel Memorial Price for Economic Science for his work – particularly notable as it was given to a psychologist, not an economist.

5. Jason Zweig, *Your Money and Your Brain: How the New Science of Neuroeconomics Can Help Make You Rich*, Souvenir Press (43 Great Russell Street, London WC1B 3PD), 2008, ISBN: 0285638084. Reproduced by kind permission of the author.

6. K. W. Eriksen and O. Kvaløy, 'Myopic investment management', *Review of Finance*, Oxford University Press for European Finance Association, 2010, 14(3): 521–42.

7. The Recency or Extrapolation Effect shows that, given a list of items to remember, we will tend to remember the last few things more than those things in the middle. We also tend to assume that items at the end of the list are of greater importance or significance. This means we tend to believe what just happened will continue to happen or is more likely to happen again.

8. E. F. Fama and K. R. French, 'Business conditions and expected returns on stocks and bonds', *Journal of Financial Economics*, November 1989, 25(1): 23–49.

9. George J. W. Goodman (born 10 August 1930) is an American economist who writes under the *nom de plume* Adam Smith (intentionally evoking the eighteenth-century Scottish economist of the same name). This quote is from *The Money Game*, Random House USA Inc., 1995, ISBN: 0394721039.

10. Nick Murray, 'Murray on marketing', *Investment Adviser Magazine*, October 1994.

11. Financial personality: by psychometric completion of profiles and/or careful questioning a trained life planner or wealth mentor can ascertain your behavioural style.

12. Our thanks to George D. Kinder for these questions.

Secret no. 7

1. Dilbert cartoon strip reproduced with permission from the Dilbert series by Scott Adams (this strip published 1 January 2008). The original version can be found at http://dilbert.com/strips/comic/2008-01-31.

2. Charles Ellis, *Winning the Loser's Game: Timeless Strategies for Successful Investing*, McGraw-Hill (PO Box 182604, Columbus, OH 43272), 2002, www.mcgraw-hill.com, ISBN: 0071387676.

3. Christopher J. Trauslen, 'Hidden fund costs every investor should know about', CFA, 22 November 2007.

4. Russel Kinnel, 'Fund spy – how fund expense ratios and star ratings predict success', Morningstar, 9 August 2010, www.morningstar.com.

Postscript

1. George Washington (22 February 1732–14 December 1799) was the first president of the United States. This quote is taken from a letter to Bushrod Washington written on 10 November 1787.

2. The figures in the Postscript are from the Finametrica Investment Risk and Return Guide, December 2012, https://www.finametrica.com/Enquiry/New.aspx.

Addendum to
Second Edition

The UK Retail Distribution Review (RDR)

From the 1st January 2013 the full affect of the Financial Services Authority (FSA) RDR came into force which effectively banned commission payments on investments. This will change the way you pay for financial advice in the future and how the costs are presented to you.

As has been discussed in the book financial and investment advice has never been free and, in the past, it was not always clear how advisers and other parties involved in the investment of your money were paid.

If you received financial advice before 1st January 2013, you would probably have paid commission to your adviser – but you might not have even known.

Initial commission was usually paid as a percentage of your

investment, typically 1 to 8%. So if you made a £10,000 investment, £100 to £800 could be paid to the adviser and reduce the money you invested. On top of this a trail commission of typically 0.5% was paid to the adviser from the annual management charge taken from the fund.

The trouble with commission was the potential for advisers to be influenced by what they would receive for recommending a particular product or using a certain provider. For example, if one investment plan paid commission of 5% some advisers might have been tempted to recommend that over one that paid them just 2%.

The new way to pay

Changes to the way advisers are paid and the information they have to give you about it have now taken effect, under the FSA RDR.

Instead of the adviser being paid commission, they now have to explain to you how much advice will cost and together you will agree how you will pay for it.

This could be charged as:

- an hourly rate;
- a set fee according to the work involved;
- a monthly retainer; or
- a percentage of the money invested.

However you pay for advice, your adviser should set out the charges in a clear and transparent way and make sure you understand how much you are paying.

The changes mean you can be sure the advice you receive will not be influenced by how much the adviser could earn from the investment. It also means that the way funds are charged has changed as the annual management charge will no longer include a trail commission payment made to the adviser (typically 0.5%) or any other payments (typically 0.25%) made to the investment platform or SIPP you use to invest through. This has meant previously "free" investment platforms now charge explicit fees for their investment administration and custody services. This will also reduce the active management annual management charge of funds going forward but is unlikely to reduce the total cost of investing with advice when the advice charges are included. It will also not reduce the cost effects of high turnover of shares within the funds, the costs of betting against the market using active management forecasting strategies or the effects of emotions on investment decisions.

Index

Notes